Y0-AVV-436

Trailering
the complete guide

Richard A. Stevens

Henry Regnery Company · Chicago

Library of Congress Cataloging in Publication Data

Stevens, Richard A
    Trailering: the complete guide

    1. Recreational vehicles. I. Title.
    GV198.7.S74   796.7'9   74-23721
    ISBN: 0-8092-8446-4
    ISBN: 0-8092-8224-0 pbk.

Drawings by George Uniacke

Copyright © 1975 by Richard A. Stevens
All rights reserved
Published by Henry Regnery Company
180 North Michigan Avenue, Chicago, Illinois 60601
Manufactured in the United States of America
Library of Congress Catalog Card Number: 74-23721
International Standard Book Number: 0-8092-8446-4

Published simultaneously in Canada by
Fitzhenry & Whiteside Limited
150 Lesmill Road
Don Mills, Ontario M3B 2T5
Canada

Contents

Introduction v

1. Trailer, Camper, or Motor Home? 1
2. New Trailer or Used? 10
3. Outfitting a Trailer 14
4. Trailering on a Budget 22
5. Hitches 27
6. Wiring 43
7. Towing Vehicles 54
8. Hooking Up 59
9. Before You Leave Home 72
10. Driving and Backing 78
11. When You Stop for the Night 86
12. Trailer Maintenance 100
13. Winterizing Your Trailer 151
14. Odds and Ends 156
15. Looking Backward and Forward 171

Index 177

Introduction

For many years we lived on Long Island and commuted to New York City. During that time we never saw—or even heard of—a travel trailer. About the closest we came to it was reading Steinbeck's *Travels with Charley*—a story of his wanderings around the United States in a camper.

In 1965, when our children had grown up and departed, my wife Kay and I decided to retire and move to California. As we drove across the country, we began to see trailers and campers on the road, and the farther west we went the more we saw.

We were mightily interested, since we loved to travel. During our working years we had taken weekend and vacation trips all over the East, and we hoped to see the West by automobile also. We were so fascinated by travel trailers that we went to the Los Angeles Trailer Show. Then we inspected all the trailers on display at the Pomona Fair.

About that time a friend gave us dozens of back issues of trailer magazines. We read every word in them, including the advertisements, and before we had finished devouring them, we were completely hooked. One important reason for our interest was financial.

Traveling around by car can be expensive. At the time we left New York, the cost of an automobile trip was about $30 to $35 per day for two people for motels, meals, gasoline, tolls, and miscellaneous traveling expenses. That was more than we could afford on retirement income, but we were beginning to see that a travel trailer might be the answer. Although we had had absolutely no experience, we thought we might be able to live and travel in a travel trailer at about the same cost as living in a house. At that time (1965) we were paying $65 per month rent for a small house, and we guessed that the cost of spaces in trailer parks and campgrounds would not be much different. Since we would prepare our own meals and sleep in our own beds, there would be no need for expensive motels and restaurants. Gasoline would cost more. Heating would cost the same or less. No telephone or water bills. Trailer insurance would add a little to the total insurance bill. Medical attention would cost the same. Upkeep on the trailer would surely be less than on a house and yard . . . . Adding it all up, we came to the conclusion that living and traveling in a travel trailer would not cost any more than staying at home. We had sold our home on Long Island, and we rented our little California house, so the travel trailer would be our only home.

We started calling on trailer dealers and making lists of features we wanted. After a few months of thinking and rethinking and changing our minds, we finally ordered a twenty-three-foot trailer with everything in it we thought we would need for full-time living. One reason we ordered a trailer that size was that it was the smallest one we could find with a separate bedroom. In smaller trailers a seat folds out or the dinette seats slide together to make a bed; you have to get out sheets, pillows, and blankets to make up your bed each night, and then you have to stow everything away in the morning before you can have breakfast. We thought that might be satisfactory for a weekend or a two-week vacation, but we didn't think we would like it as a steady diet.

Another consideration, since we intended to live in our trailer indefinitely, was the additional storage space for both winter and summer clothing. In fact, since we were to have no other home, everything we owned had to be stored either in the trailer or the car. After ordering the trailer, we traded in our small car for one that would pull the 6,500-pound load.

Then came the thrill of our first trailer trip—to Lake Mead. The nervousness we felt disappeared almost as soon as we were on the road. The February sun was bright and warm at Boulder Campground, right on the shore of the lake. Each campsite was separated from the next by a thick growth of oleanders, so each trailer had its own private spot. After a delightful four-day vacation, we took a leisurely trip home, stopping overnight in Barstow—our first overnight stop in a trailer park.

Our plan was to take a number of short shakedown cruises before embarking on any long trips, so that we would get some practical experience. We were unsure of what we would and would not need, we wanted more driving experience and practice in backing, and we had to learn how to pack both car and trailer. And we didn't want to be too far away from the dealer in case some unexpected trouble developed. After that, if all went well, we expected to set out on a long trip around the country that would last a year, or two, or more.

After Lake Mead we took trips to Ventura and to Carpentería State Park on the beach, where we had the ocean pounding in almost at our doorstep. Then we crossed the Mojave Desert to Furnace Creek Campground in Death Valley, which we explored from one end to the other. We went to Salton Sea, that amazing body of water in the southern California desert. We went to Parker, Arizona, on the Colorado River, to Phoenix and Tucson, to Mesa and Tombstone, to Nogales and Yuma, and back through Indio, where most of the dates in the United States are grown.

In the summer we ventured a bit farther. We spent a month in Sequoia National Park and King's Canyon, high in the Sierras, where we caught trout in the cold mountain streams. After a week in Fresno, we drove to San Francisco to visit our eldest son.

We went to Dogwood Campground in the San Bernardino Mountains, to Joshua Tree National Monument, and to Shaver Lake in the high Sierras with our grandchildren. By this time we thought we were ready for a longer trip.

We went up the coast to Washington and the Olympic Peninsula. Then we crossed the United States several times and toured Canada. Eight years later we are still at it.

From the time we saw our first travel trailer, questions kept popping into our heads. Are they hard to pull? How do you hook them to a car? What do you do about electricity and water and sewers? Are they insulated? What is the smallest trailer that has everything in it that we would need? How does the propane gas system work, and how long will a tank of gas last? Reading the trailer magazines answered some questions, but the more we learned, the more questions we had. We sent away for some trailer books, which proved to be worthless, so we had to learn by trial and error—and, more importantly, from other trailerites. Everywhere we went we met friendly, experienced trailerites who answered our questions and taught us hundreds of trailering details. But it took a long time to get most of our questions answered.

The purpose of this book is to pass on to you what we have learned in eight years of full-time trailering. You won't find a travelogue or information on where to go—there are hundreds of books and pamphlets and magazines that will do that for you. You will find information that will help you decide what kind of recreational vehicle to buy, what you will need to outfit it, and what it will cost. You will find out a good deal about hitches, electrical connections, trailer plumbing, and a great many other things that will save your headaches.

Since all things mechanical need maintenance and repairs, the book includes a substantial section on keeping trailer appliances in good working order. Although the explanations are detailed, you will find nothing difficult or very technical, and most explanations are accompanied by helpful diagrams or illustrations.

Perhaps you can use some of the information immediately, but, in any case, you can keep the book in a handy place for future reference.

As we have been helped so often by fellow trailerites, we hope this book will contribute to your trailering safety and happiness.

1

Trailer, Camper, or Motor Home?

THE FIRST QUESTION that needs a good deal of thought is how you will use your recreation vehicle. Will you use it for weekends, vacations, and long trips, or will you be living in it full-time? As you already know, a trailer is pulled behind a tow car, but campers and motor homes are self-propelled. The camper is usually a little shelter that is built separately and then slid into the back of a pickup truck. But there are also chassis-mount campers that are built permanently right onto the truck frame. The motor home is usually built on a longer chassis, like a bus, and the driver's seat is part of the interior living space. Then there are all kinds of variations, with all kinds of trade names, in all kinds of sizes, some with the most elaborate equipment, some with almost none.

    Each type has its advantages and its disadvantages. It takes a little time and effort to hook up and unhook a trailer. But once you are unhooked, your tow car is available for sight-seeing, shopping, and side trips, just as it would be at home. Although campers and motor homes are not hooked up to a tow vehicle, every time you use them you have to unhook utility connections and connect them again when you return. Another consideration is that most campers and motor homes are a bit unwieldy to use as a family car.

The self-propelled vehicles have the advantage of being able to travel roads that would not be practical for most trailers. And it is easier to back a camper or motor home than a car and trailer.

If you are going to the woods or to the beach for weekends, or if you are going on a two-week vacation and will be traveling from place to place every day, it seems to us that a camper or a motor home would best suit your needs. On the other hand, if you need something you can live in for long periods, you would probably be happier with a trailer. In our case, since we planned to live in it full-time, there was no question about our selection of a trailer.

Travel Trailers

For those who are as unfamiliar with trailers as we were, we pause for a short description. Travel trailers come in all sizes and shapes, from twelve feet long to over thirty, and with equipment varying from a bed and a stove to the most elaborate furnishings. Ours was 23 feet long by 8 feet wide (Figure 1). Dinette across the front, four-burner range on the left, then a double sink and kitchen cabinets. Across the aisle a gas/electric refrigerator and space heater. A doorway opened into the bedroom, which consisted of a double bed, dressing table, drawers, and wardrobe. A television set on a movable platform could be seen from either the dinette or the bedroom. At the rear of the bedroom a sliding door opened into a little bathroom with a clothes closet, wash basin, toilet, and shower.

Two propane bottles outside supplied gas for cooking, heating, refrigeration, hot water, and gas light. A large storage battery supplied power for lights, ceiling and stove vent fans, Monomatic toilet, and compressor for water tank. We could live comfortably for a week or ten days on battery power, and for three weeks on two bottles of propane in cold

Trailer, Camper, or Motor Home? 3

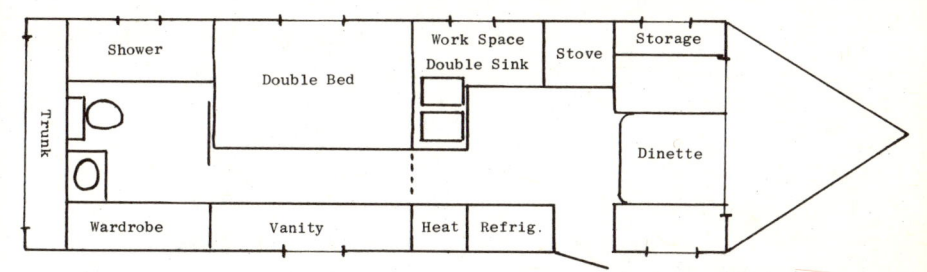

Fig. 1. Floor plan of our first 23-foot trailer. Not shown are kitchen cabinets over the stove, work space, and sink; storage space under dinette seats and bed; drawers in vanity, under sink, and work space; and a bunk bed over dinette.

weather (much longer in summer), so we often stayed in campgrounds where there was no electricity. In cities and towns we stayed in trailer parks where we could connect to electricity, water, and sewers.

Camper Plus Small Car

Some people tow a small car, like a Volkswagen or Jeep, behind their camper. Then at their destination they live in their camper or motor home and use the small car for local transportation. The small car is much cheaper to operate and more convenient. The negatives are the upkeep, licensing, depreciation, and maintenance of two cars—which can be expensive. And with a small car on the back of the camper or motor home it is all but impossible to back the rig more than a few feet. In the first place, you can't see the narrower car in the back; but even if you could, the longer wheel base of the tow vehicle makes it turn so much slower than the quick-turning small car that it is almost impossible to control it. If you have to back any distance or around a corner, the only solution is to unhook the small car and back it separately.

If you find a suitable spot in a crowded campground, you don't like to move your camper out of it for fear that someone else will move in. This is a minor problem, as most campers leave a chair or sign to reserve their space. Other campers and trailerites are almost always very nice people (with few exceptions) who respect the notice. In some campgrounds, spaces are reserved.

Others load a scooter or motorcycle on the back of their camper for local transportation. That is great for some—especially young people—but it would not be acceptable for older people like us, particularly in bad weather. Another drawback is that motorcycles and trail bikes are not allowed in a growing number of campgrounds because they are noisy and can tear up the terrain.

People who live in a city might decide on a camper or motor home because they have no place to store a trailer. There are local ordinances in some cities, towns, and counties regarding the parking of recreational vehicles of all kinds. It would be wise to find out about local rules and regulations before you buy.

People who travel with the weather usually choose a trailer because they can park it for the winter down south and for the summer up north. For those on Social Security it is an economical and pleasant way to live. Senior citizens who have neither the money nor the energy to travel all the time can park their trailers in trailer parks for a reasonable rental and stay for months at a time.

Some retired people visit their children and grandchildren for weeks or months. We love to visit our children, and they like to have us. But we enjoy living in our own trailer home, sleeping in our own beds, using our own bathroom, and cooking most of our meals. That way, neither family is inconvenienced, and frictions have little chance to develop.

Suppose you narrow your choice to a trailer—there are still lots of decisions to make. There are tiny trailers, tent trailers, big 30-footers, and everything in between.

Tent Trailers

If you are young, you may want to consider a tent trailer. Sometimes they are called *tent campers*, or *pop-ups*, but they really are trailers. Like their brothers, they come in different sizes and degrees of luxury. All of them fold down into a comparatively small box and are light enough to be pulled by a passenger car with a simple hitch—not necessarily a frame hitch. Since they are light, they require no brakes of their own, and since they are so small, they cause almost no sway. The only connections needed between car and trailer are for running lights and stop and turn signals. Wiring for these is easily installed.

Some pop-ups take quite a while to set up for the night, while others have automatic electric and hydraulic devices for raising the top—they really do pop up.

Some have canvas tents, others have plastic tops and canvas sides, and a few are plastic. In all of them, the beds fold out to make a surprising amount of sleeping space, several feet off the ground. You can get tent trailers with propane tanks, cook stoves, refrigerators or ice boxes, lights, and considerable storage space. We have seen some expensive models that were almost luxurious. But we must tell you that we have no experience with tent campers; we have only looked at them. Pop-ups would not be the choice of many older people or retirees. Like us, they would not like the inconvenience of putting up the tent in the rain and folding it down again in bad weather. They would probably want a few more comforts and more storage space.

But pop-ups have great advantages for young couples and families. As a matter of fact, we have noticed in our travels that practically all of the tent-trailer people are young. They can travel during their vacations and see the country at a fraction of the cost of staying in motels and eating in restaurants, and they can enjoy camping life at the same time. In addition to the national and state parks and forests, there are now thousands of private parks and campgrounds all over the United States where a family can stay overnight for $3 or $4. Most of these campgrounds have hot showers included in the price, and many of them have swimming pools and playgrounds for the children. There are still many national forests where primitive camping is free.

Small Trailer or Large?

If you are older, you will probably be interested in a bit

more comfort. But before you decide on any particular size or kind of trailer, we would like to suggest that you have a good hitch put on your car and then rent a trailer and take some trips in it before you decide which kind to get. When you do decide—no matter what kind of trailer you buy—be sure to take off the wheels and see that they are properly greased—or have the dealer do it. A good dealer will check the wheels as a matter of routine—but be sure he does it.

Our first trailer was 23 feet long—longer than most people buy the first time. But we later traded it in for a 30-footer. New trailer owners almost always select a smaller size because they are hesitant about towing a longer one. And nine times out of ten, they will trade it in for a longer one later on, after they get used to towing the smaller one. In our case, we found little difference between towing the 23-foot and the 30-foot trailers.

The longer the trailer, the easier it is to back it. The shorter the trailer, the quicker it turns, so the easier it is to jackknife. But the longer turning radius of the longer trailers makes them unsuitable for mountain roads with sharp turns and switchbacks. And the heavier weight of the larger trailers means that it is necessary to have a lot more power in your tow car or truck. Low-powered cars can pull almost any size trailer easily enough if the road is flat and there is no wind against you. But with an under-powered car, when you start up hill your troubles also start. The engine may overheat, and you risk blowing your transmission.

Automobile manufacturers publish tables showing the kind of engine, transmission, tires, rear-end ratio, and so on needed to pull trailers of various weights. There are so many types of cars and trucks and so many specifications that it would not be practical to reprint all such data here. The information is readily available from car and truck dealers. But one word of caution. Trailer manufacturers list the weights of their trailers in their literature, or dealers will tell you the weight of each trailer. This weight is always much smaller than the actual weight of the trailer on the road.

In the first place, there are various options that you can

Trailer, Camper, or Motor Home? 7

order which will increase the weight of the trailer, such as an air conditioner, overhead bunk beds, larger tires, spare tire rack, battery, and so forth. Then before you even start loading the trailer you put water in the water tank, water heater, and toilet. A 30-gallon water tank, at 8 pounds per gallon, adds 240 pounds; a 9-gallon water heater adds 72 more, plus whatever amount is in the holding tank. When you fill your propane tanks, two 30-pound tanks add 60 more pounds. So water and propane can add 300 to 500 pounds to the weight of your trailer.

Our 23-foot trailer was rated by the manufacturer as weighing 3,800 pounds. We added larger tires and an overhead bunk. In addition to the usual food and clothing, since we are full-time trailerites, we carried both summer and winter clothes, a complete line of medicines and bathroom supplies, and a larger-than-usual number of tools, fix-it supplies, and materials. When we put our trailer on the public scales, it weighed 6,500 pounds—an increase of 2,700 pounds over manufacturer's weight. Approximately 700 pounds was added by the bunk bed, larger tires, water, and propane; therefore, the trailer must have weighed 4,500 pounds before it was loaded. That leaves 2,000 pounds as the weight of the clothing, food on the shelves and in the refrig-

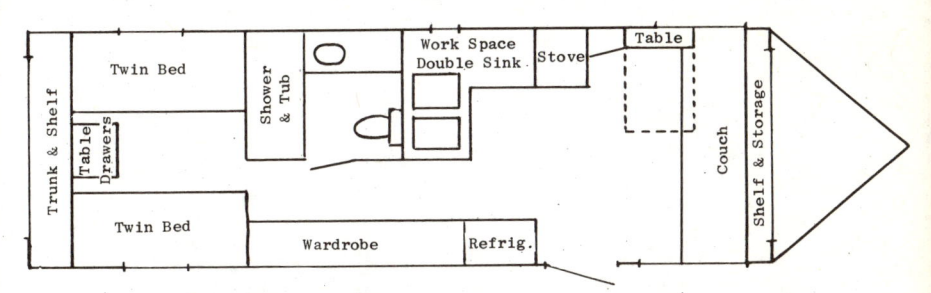

Fig. 2. Our second trailer, 30 feet long, had about the same storage space as our 23-footer but much more living space. Not shown: storage behind and under front couch; kitchen cabinets over sinks, work space, and stove; cabinets, clothes hamper under basin, and medicine cabinet in bathroom; storage under and over beds. Space between stove and table is a bookcase. Table drops flat against wall when not in use; 3 extra leaves allow table to be extended to seat six comfortably.

erator, books, tools, and all other personal possessions.

We have about the same amount of storage space in our present 30-footer as we did in the 23-foot trailer. The difference is in living space, not storage space (Figure 2). The manufacturer's weight on our present trailer is 5,985 pounds. We added an air conditioner, larger refrigerator, and storm windows—about 200 pounds more. With water and propane, we had about 560 additional pounds. When we loaded about 2,000 pounds into the trailer, the total came to about 8,500 pounds, and that's just what it weighed on the scales.

Anyhow, that will give you the general idea—your trailer is going to weigh quite a lot more than you might think if you didn't figure it out. And while we're on the subject, the tongue is going to weigh more, too; that is, more weight is going to be carried by your car than the listed tongue weight of the trailer. So get a heavier hitch and be sure the suspension and tires on your tow car are heavy enough to handle the additional weight. We will cover this more thoroughly in the chapter on hitches.

Plate 1. Looking toward the front of our trailer. We are expecting dinner guests. After dinner, the table will fold flat against the wall, and we will be in the "parlor."

Trailer, Camper, or Motor Home? 9

Plate 2. Photo taken from the front couch. Door in the hallway opens into the bathroom. Bedroom is at the rear.

Plate 3. Our trailer

2

New Trailer or Used?

If you decide you want a very specific kind of trailer with very specific extras, you will probably not be able to find what you want secondhand. But if you are willing to make your choice from a somewhat more limited selection, you can save quite a lot of money by buying a used trailer. You might even get one that is *better* than new. When we traded in our first trailer, it had been used a year and a half and had traveled 12,000 miles. It was a much better trailer than it had been when we bought it. All the bugs and imperfections had been corrected, and many improvements had been added. As to the mileage, a trailer can be expected to last almost indefinitely if you take care of it and keep the wheels greased, so the 12,000 miles were almost nothing. We have talked with many people who have bought secondhand trailers at bargain prices, simply because trailers have a book value, like automobiles. The real worth of a trailer has very little to do with the book value. As a matter of fact, some of the older trailers are better built than some of the newer ones that cost a lot more.

There are several reasons for good used trailers to come on the market. Older retirees find that they are no longer able to travel because of age or illness. Widows are often left with a trailer they can't use, since they seldom travel alone. As previously mentioned, people frequently trade in a smaller trailer for a larger one; and sometimes, after purchasing a recreation vehicle, the owner decides it is the wrong kind for him and trades it in or sells it while it is still almost new.

The chances of getting a better-than-new used trailer are very good. When you buy a new trailer you also buy all kinds of imperfections, just as you do when you buy a new car—only worse. If there is any such thing as a new trailer in perfect or near-perfect condition, we have never heard of it. The trailer manufacturing business is highly competitive, and in this day of continuously rising costs for labor and materials, manufacturers are always on the lookout for ways to cut corners in order to keep their selling price competitive. Of course, we are not closely familiar with every trailer on the market. There are hundreds of them, and from time to time we see new models we have never seen before. No doubt there are manufacturers who will disagree with us or say that they are an exception. Maybe so. It's possible. But our experience, and that of hundreds of trailer owners with whom we have talked all over the country, is that trailers are delivered to dealers in imperfect condition. They come off the assembly line and off they go with little or no inspection. We've seen trailers come in to a dealer's lot littered with sawdust and metal shavings, and with scraps of materials all over, under, and in every place imaginable inside the trailer. A busy dealer will clean it up enough to make it presentable, but the litter will still be under the bed and behind the compressor—and this is true of expensive trailers as well as the cheaper ones.

But litter is the least of your worries—there will probably be many things that need fixing or adjusting. For example, in our first trailer, purchased in 1966, we had the following problems:

(1) We ordered a holding tank along with the recirculating

toilet. It was delivered without the holding tank. The dealer arranged for a man to come from the factory to install it.

(2) The drain from the wash basin in the bathroom emptied into the holding tank instead of into the sewer outlet. The result was that the holding tank filled up quickly, leaving no room to dump the toilet. The manufacturer refused to fix it, so we had the drain rerouted ourselves.

(3) The shower curtain was too narrow and short, so that water dripped outside the shower onto the floor. We replaced it with a new curtain and a longer rod.

(4) One of the wheel spring hangers was cracked and almost severed. Fortunately I discovered it while greasing the shackle bolts and had it welded before we had an accident.

(5) The thermostat for the space heater was faulty. We returned it to the factory, and they sent us a new one.

(6) Wheel wells were not insulated. Since we expected to be in cold weather, we bought plywood and insulation and installed it ourselves.

(7) The gas stove had no shut-off valve. We installed a valve and fittings ourselves.

(8) There were a great many places where plywood and molding had separated or plywood had come loose. Doors, drawers, and window screens fitted poorly. The dinette table was screwed on crooked, and so forth. All these things were repaired before the trailer was traded in.

In addition to fixing things that were wrong, we added a number of improvements. Had we known that we were going to keep the trailer only a year and a half, we might not have put so much work and cash into it. Here is a list of the improvements we made:

Drapes for doorway to bedroom
Towel racks and shelves
Cup hooks (the kind that prevent cups from bouncing out)
Under-the-trailer wires in plastic tubing
Undercoating (The aluminum sheeting under the trailer was full of staple holes, so we had the entire bottom undercoated.)

12-volt wiring and switch to reverse the direction of recirculating toilet filter (This is now standard equipment, but was not at that time.)
Aluminum clothes hooks
Aluminum edging and plywood for bookcase
Insulated metal ceiling above space heater, aluminum duct between walls, rheostat and squirrel-cage blower, duct to bedroom and bathroom, and wiring—for blower system to take hot air above the furnace and blow it along the floor
Movable bed extension to increase bed width to standard 54-inch double-bed size
Materials to make bed extension for dinette bed (removable) to make it 54 inches wide
Ozite carpet and rubber underlay throughout
Traverse rod and curtain in front of bunk bed (We carried so much gear on the bunk we decided to hide it with curtains.)
Pure-O-Vac (Our recirculating toilet was so smelly we installed this device—a squirrel-cage fan that exhausts the air in the bowl to the outside.)

We installed everything ourselves. I hate to think what it would have cost if we had had to pay for labor. We would have spent well over another thousand dollars. When you consider that we sold the trailer for a thousand dollars less than we paid for it, you can see why we say you can get a real bargain on a used trailer.

3

Outfitting a Trailer

Our first new trailer, purchased in 1966, cost $4,292.67. By 1974 trailer prices had increased 33 to 50 percent over 1966 prices, and they are likely to go even higher. Our 1966 price included tax and the following extras:

Bunk bed over dinette
Double insulation
Front fiberglass awning
12-volt electrical system with converter and regular 110-volt system
Storm windows
Water purifier
Heavy-duty tires (7.00 x 15, 8-ply rating)
Spare tire and wheel
TV shelf
Rotating TV antenna and jack
Ceiling fans
Back-up lights
4-wheel electric brakes
Monomatic toilet
Large holding tank

Lined drapes
Heavy-duty battery
8-gallon (30-pound) propane tanks and regulator

But the actual cost of getting it on the road was a good deal more than that. We bought it in California, so the license was expensive, $75.00. In most states licenses cost much less.

Then came the matter of outfitting it. The easiest way to give you an idea of what you might need is to list what we bought.

Sheets and pillow cases
2 good dry chemical fire extinguishers, one for front and one for rear
25 feet of electrical wire and supplies to connect trailer to house electricity
Rubber to line shelves
Bedspread
2 plastic trays for silverware
Plastic bucket
Paper towel holder
Rubber-covered dish racks
Dish towel ring
Hydrometer to test battery charge
Set of reflectors to put on road in case of road trouble
Spare 12-volt interior light bulb
Tea kettle
Spare mantles for propane lights
2 folding chairs
Clothesline cord
Cooking pans and containers
2 plastic cups
5 padlocks, all using the same key, for locking hitch, sewer hose tube, aluminum ladder on rack under trailer, and 2 spares
Lug wrench (We later bought a larger one.)
Rubber floor mat
Plastic refrigerator containers
Ironing board cover

Tow chain, in case of road trouble
Battery jumper cables
70 feet of wire to use as a radio aerial
Coleman single-burner lantern
Gasoline can (for white gas for lantern fuel)
Hibachi for cooking outdoors
Extra Coleman mantles
Thin foam rubber, about ⅛ inch thick, which can be bought in variety stores (We cut it into strips and wrapped it around wire coat hangers, so that the wire was completely covered. This keeps the clothes on the hanger and keeps them from wearing out from rubbing on the wire while moving.)
Canvas for propane tank covers (We made our own.)
Rubber dish drainer
Small rug
Grease gun for greasing shackle bolts under the trailer (Many trailers now pack the spring hangers with rubber, so greasing is not necessary.)
Tube of grease
Rubber floor mat
1½-ton hydraulic jack to lift the axle in case of a flat
Ice tray for refrigerator
Batteries for radio
Bicycle pump and hose (various uses, including pressurizing water tank in case compressor stops working)
2 sewer hose clamps
Sewer connector fitting
50 feet of plastic water hose for drinking water
2 fly swatters
Bug spray
Enameled pan
Can opener, hand type
Dust pan
Scouring brush
Evaporative cooler (Since this trailer did not have air conditioning, we bought a small cooler that fit perfectly against the bedroom window. In the Southwest we have been in heat as high as 112°, and this little gem kept the bedroom cool and comfortable. Evaporative coolers will not cool properly unless humidity is very low.)

Outfitting a Trailer 17

Thermometer
Melmac dinnerware
Ax
Cooking grid for use over campfire
Yellow electric bulb for outside use, to avoid attracting bugs
Wire and clamp-on for outside light
Toilet-cleaning brush
Hurricane candles in a glass so that they don't blow out
5-gallon water jug (We later found that two 3-gallon jugs were better and easier to handle.)
Two 25-foot electrical cords
Plastic pouring pipe (This device was inserted in the water-filling pipe and prevented the water from backing up if we poured it too fast. It made filling the tank much faster and easier.)
Extra filter for water purifier
Waterless hand cleaner, available at supermarkets and auto stores (After you have finished hooking up, it is easy to clean your hands with waterless cleaner before you get in the car.)
Wire and connections for installing TV
Battery clock
12-inch Zenith TV
Inverter for converting 12-volt DC battery current into 110-volt AC house current
Extra bed sheet
Sauce pan
Sponge-rubber tape to weatherproof door
Sewer hose sleeve to add an extra length of hose
15 feet of high-pressure water hose
18 feet of heat tape to keep water hose from freezing
Hub cap for spare tire
Electric heater
Heavy electric cord
Plywood and other materials for table top (We made a larger top to fit over the dinette table when we had company.)
Flour sifter
More plastic dishes
Awning frame and awning
Carbon dioxide fire extinguisher, secondhand (We already had the dry chemical type.)

Chair casters
Plastic bowls
25-foot extra water hose
Additional sewer hose, sleeve, and clamps
Night light
Toothbrush holder for bathroom

That's about it for outfitting the trailer. We have listed items in considerable detail to remind you of things you might forget.

But that is still not quite all. There are additional tools and supplies you will need if you are going to do much trailering. You will find yourself in places where things are not readily available without going long distances. We already had many of these items, and you probably do, too. Here is a list of additional supplies you may need for long-term trailering:

More than one flashlight (at least one big one and spare batteries)
White glue, plastic wood, plastic repair cement, tube of clear or aluminum silicone rubber
Distilled water for battery
Spool of No. 12 flexible automotive wire for 12-volt connections and repair; length of lamp cord for 110 volts
Electrical connectors or wire nuts in assorted sizes and plastic electrical tape; spare fuses of each kind used in the trailer and spare 20-ampere fuses and Fustats in case you blow a fuse in the trailer park (A couple of spare in-line 12-volt fuse holders sometimes come in handy.)
Radio batteries
Lengths of ¼-inch and ⅜-inch copper tubing and a few spare ferrules (compression rings). (Tubing connections are made either with ferrules or by flaring the ends of the tubing. If you have flared connections, you will need a flaring tool, which is not expensive.)
Spare faucet washers
An assortment of screws, nails, washers, lock washers, small bolts and nuts, cotter pins, sheet metal screws—especially hex-head no. 8, 1 inch or ¾ inch long—which are used to put the siding on most trailers

Outfitting a Trailer

- Paint (We take rust-proof primer, aluminum paint, and a can of paint or lacquer to match the color of the trailer. The trailer tongue and rear bumper get nicked in traveling, and we touch them up occasionally. We also take a few brushes, old rags, and a quart of paint thinner.)
- A small roll of duct tape, which can be used for all kinds of repairs
- Can of light household lubricating oil and a can of SAE-20 oil
- Brickettes and lighter fluid for cooking outdoors
- White gas for your lantern, in a metal can (In some states it is against the law for a dealer to fill plastic containers with gasoline.)
- Tube of aluminum roofing compound and a roll of putty tape
- A few small pieces of sheet metal for making repairs
- Can of Liquid Wrench (excellent for getting frozen nuts off)
- Various-sized fittings for sewer connections and some extra 3-inch hose clamps. Also some small-sized hose clamps for water hose and smaller rubber tubing
- Hose Y with shutoff valve on at least one branch for connecting two hoses to one faucet
- Ball of twine and length of rope
- Ant traps (These are little metal stakes with a container of ant poison attached to the top. We have been in a number of places where ants find their way inside. The traps are stuck in the ground next to the wheels, jack post, water and sewer hoses, and electrical cable. They work beautifully.)
- Valve cores (We carry a few spares for the tires and pressurized water tank. To keep these where we can find them, along with small bolts, screws, fittings, mantles, and other small things, we carry a little case of drawers—the kind that is sold in hardware and discount stores.)
- Baking soda (For removing bug stains, we have never found anything better than baking soda moistened with water and rubbed with a soft cloth—and it doesn't rub off the enamel. It is also good for small specks of road tar. For large splotches of tar, moisten the rag with paint thinner or kerosene.)

In addition to supplies listed above, we also carry a lot of tools, since working with them is a hobby with us. We enjoy fixing things, not only ours, but our neighbors' in trailer parks and campgrounds. You will find people like that everywhere you go, so even if you are not handy with tools yourself, you are likely to find someone who will be glad to give you a hand.

Here are some of the most useful tools for the do-it-yourself trailerite:

- 8-inch and 6-inch crescent wrenches
- Set of small wrenches, from $3/16$-inch to $1/2$-inch size for working on things like your water heater and refrigerator
- Large channel lock pliers that open to about 4 inches
- Test lights for both battery and house current
- Set of short and long screwdrivers for both large and small screws, Phillips and standard (Some trailers use odd screw heads, like clutch heads, which are shaped like little figure eights. And there are screws with square indentations. You can get both kinds in several sizes at hardware stores.)
- Knife and sharpening stone
- Regular pliers, electrical pliers with cutters, water pump pliers, and locking pliers
- Punch
- Hammer
- ¼-inch hex-head nut driver
- Hand drill like a Yankee drill and a set of various-sized drill bits (An electric drill is fine, but you will be in places where electricity is not available.)
- Short-handled shovel (very necessary if you get stuck)
- Small hacksaw for cutting metal
- A small wood saw (A keyhole saw will save space.)
- Metal-cutting shears
- Assorted brushes, including old toothbrushes

There are many other tools you could have, of course, but this is about the minimum list for use in and around a trailer. Besides that, you need car tools, which you probably already have.

If you are the handyman type, you might be interested in some of the other tools we carry:

¼-inch and ½-inch electric drills, with twist drills from ⅛-inch to 1-inch, flat drills for wood, a set of number drills from no. 1 to no. 60, and a set of letter drills

6½-inch portable power saw with combination and plywood blades

Heavy duty sander and sanding belts

Saber saw and assorted blades

Router and bits

Putty knives, caulking gun, block plane, ballpeen and 2-pound hammer, offset screw drivers, pocket and 25-foot tape measure, wood chisels, cold chisels

Two portable vises

C-clamps—a dozen or so, from 1-inch to 6-inch size

Two handsaws and a backsaw

Propane torch, electric soldering irons, large copper iron, solder, and flux

Set of Allen wrenches, complete set of open-end and box wrenches, and socket wrenches with ½-inch and ¼-inch drives

Ice picks, center punches, drift punches, grinding wheels to fit the electric drills, nail sets, countersinks for metal and wood, pop rivet tool, and rivets of various sizes of both steel and aluminum

Two pry bars, scroll saw, grommet-setting tool, sheet metal hand bending tool, scribers, squares and T-squares, compass, dividers, brace and screwdriver blades

Small pipe wrench and pipe and tubing cutters

2 collapsible saw horses and 2 boards to lay on top of them to make a workbench

4

Trailering on a Budget

OUR GOOD FRIENDS fall into two categories: those who think we are nuts and those who like to travel. The first question people who are interested in traveling and trailering ask is "How much does it cost?"

Like most of our friends, we have to count the cost, too. We have Social Security (but no pension), cash from selling our home, and some not-very-large savings. So we have kept records of all expenditures with a budget system we started many years ago. We know how much we spent and what we spent it for. In the figures we give below, everything is included except the original cost of the car, the original cost of the trailer, and income taxes.

For the last seven years our expenses for *everything* (including all medical and dental expenses, insurance, food, entertainment, gifts, rent, travel expenses, upkeep and improvements on car and trailer) have varied from a low of $4,226.50 to a high of $5,658.58. Our car averaged 16,000 miles per year, and we have pulled our trailer an average of 6,000 miles per year.

You can see that we actually pulled the trailer only about 30 days per year—less than 10 percent of the days. When we came to a place we liked, we stayed for a few days, for a week or two, or longer. When we visited our children, we rented a spot in a trailer park and stayed for a few weeks or a few months. One time we stayed in Tucson for six months. Last year we stayed in the Rio Grande Valley all winter. We spent several winters in Florida.

The variations in the size of the expenditures from one year to the next depend on how much traveling we did (gasoline and car maintenance), medical expenses, and how much we spent for improvements. Those are the items that varied the most. Our biggest expenses are insurance (car, trailer, and health) and groceries, which do not vary much, and automobile expenses, which vary considerably. Trailer maintenance fluctuated widely, depending on what we decided to spend on improvements.

The chart shows our list of expenses for seven years of traveling.

From conversations with many other trailerites and from our own observations, we think our expenditures are somewhere near the average. Many people live on considerably less, and many spend a good deal more. But our purpose is to answer your questions about how much trailering costs, and you can adjust our figures as necessary, depending on your own circumstances and allowing for price increases.

Explanation of Budget Items

Automobile. All maintenance costs, including tires and gasoline. We purchased a new truck in January 1971, and several hundred dollars of the 1971 costs were for materials to build the inside of the camper (bunks, storage cabinets, Porta Potti, etc.).

Trailer Maintenance. Items such as tools, nails, glue, pots and pans, kitchen curtains, welcome mat, night light, mail box, thermometer, silicone polish, chair webbing, paint, trailer license, fixing a flat, sheets and pillow cases, curtain linings, frying pan, grease for trailer wheels, masking tape, thermos bottle, and, of course, major expenses like an evaporative cooler on the roof, an inverter, and an awning.

In July of 1967 we bought our new 30-foot trailer, so the $759 that year includes the cost of fixing it up and outfitting it.

In 1969 we decided on a lot of other improvements, including Mylar screens for the bedroom, battery charger, Water Pic, 12-volt fluorescent light, aluminum ladder under the trailer, the swamp cooler in addition to the air conditioner, air pressure tank, and a great many other less expensive improvements, like a light-dimmer switch.

In 1971 we bought new trailer tires for $200, changed the hitch socket from a 2-inch to a $2^5/_{16}$-inch size, and spent several hundred dollars for a storage shed for our Florida trailer park space.

Travel Expenses. In 1967 these expenses included some overnight trailer park charges that are listed as rent in all other years. Includes tolls, parking, Golden Eagle pass, atlas and other maps, AAA dues, trailer park books, and in 1969 the cost of an airplane trip.

Clothing. These expenses are low because we are still wearing clothes we had when we retired and because we now need very little in the way of good clothes.

Gifts. Christmas and birthday presents and all contributions to charities.

Entertaining and Visiting. This category includes anything we do for entertainment, including dinners and lunches out. Not very high because we don't care to eat out particularly, and because we quickly learned to pass up tourist traps. But we do not pass up things like a visit to Butchart Gardens on Vancouver Island or Carlsbad Caverns.

Electricity and Gas. Expenses for propane and electricity in trailer parks. The cost of both varies widely from place to place.

Household Expenses. This category includes all food, grocery items like soap and detergents, and minor drug items such as toothpaste and shampoo.

Insurance. Premiums for car, trailer, Blue Cross and

Budgets: 1967–1973

	1967	1968	1969	1970	1971	1972	1973
Automobile	$ 955.23	$1,370.08	$ 730.64	$ 851.15	$1,482.03	$ 508.32	$ 795.53
Trailer Maintenance	759.86	378.09	699.19	327.79	767.51	546.22	543.27
Travel Expenses	255.50	96.39	181.41	61.07	67.90	26.08	83.25
Clothing	49.30	64.10	72.05	59.67	28.03	67.45	86.64
Gifts	234.07	220.25	229.14	236.94	313.39	344.31	378.16
Entertaining, Visiting	87.87	143.15	52.80	129.89	139.74	144.84	231.67
Electricity, Propane	114.80	84.47	158.86	136.73	191.73	167.08	111.64
Household Expenses	958.55	971.34	1,049.78	1,040.72	1,057.08	1,095.16	1,165.32
Insurance	556.80	692.25	634.05	453.25	587.90	494.80	489.60
Medical	163.99	131.64	515.79	306.64	292.04	309.77	279.21
Telephone	38.95	15.15	35.70	33.20	27.85	67.36	53.74
Rent	273.63	562.55	401.23	372.57	417.29	403.45	436.43
Miscellaneous	132.00	124.31	361.65	217.04	286.09	275.11	316.38
Totals	$4,575.55	$4,853.77	$5,122.29	$4,226.50	$5,658.58	$4,499.95	$4,970.84

major medical insurance. Some of the variation depends on whether premiums are paid in January or December. (Does not include Medicare payments, which we treat as a deduction from Social Security income.) We carry more insurance than most people we have talked with, on the theory that the less you can afford it, the more you need it. Our only concern has been that if severe illness did strike, the enormous cost could wipe us out. If either of us had a prolonged illness and then went on our last trip, the other would be left without enough to live on, and we would not be happy being a burden to our children and their families.

Medical. All doctors' fees, dental work, medicines, pain relievers, and so forth.

Telephone. All charges for telephone calls.

Rent. Fees for overnight stops in campgrounds or trailer parks.

Miscellaneous. This category includes items such as haircuts, reading matter, stamps, and anything that did not fall under another category.

5

Hitches

TRAILERS ARE GENERALLY hooked to the tow car by means of a steel ball on the back of the towing vehicle that fits into a socket on the front of the trailer. There is also a relatively new type of trailer, misnamed *fifth wheeler*, which has a bottom section of the front of the trailer cut out so that it fits up over the back of a pickup truck or over the top of an automobile. We will briefly discuss fifth wheelers, but first let's examine the more conventional type of hitch, the type used for about 98 percent of all travel trailers.

For the average travel trailer, the ball is 2 inches in diameter; for the larger trailers, the ball is 2-$5/16$ inches in diameter. (Tent campers and boat trailers have smaller ones.) A clamp holds the socket on the ball, and a lever can be lifted to release the clamp so that the socket can be lifted from the ball. This clamp is strong enough that you can jack up the front of your trailer and it will raise the rear of the car. When you are ready to tow, the lever can be locked down (we use a padlock) so that the socket can't possibly bounce off the ball while traveling.

28 TRAILERING

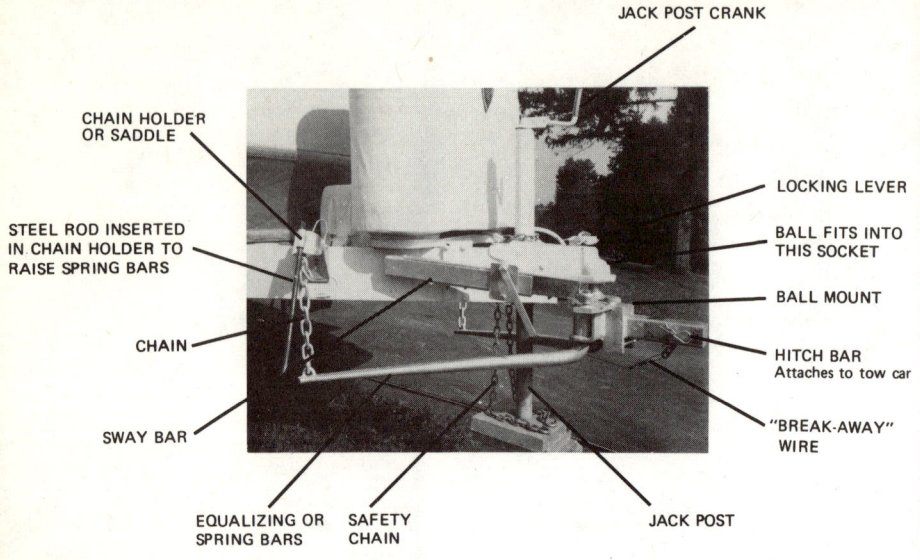

Photo labels:
- JACK POST CRANK
- CHAIN HOLDER OR SADDLE
- LOCKING LEVER
- STEEL ROD INSERTED IN CHAIN HOLDER TO RAISE SPRING BARS
- BALL FITS INTO THIS SOCKET
- BALL MOUNT
- CHAIN
- HITCH BAR Attaches to tow car
- SWAY BAR
- "BREAK-AWAY" WIRE
- EQUALIZING OR SPRING BARS
- SAFETY CHAIN
- JACK POST

Plate 4. Trailer hitch

Equalizing Hitches

Unless the trailer is very small and light, you will need leveling bars to lift the back of the tow car and throw more weight onto the front wheels. This device is called an equalizing hitch, and it works like this (Figure 3):

(1) When you lower the trailer hitch onto the tow-car ball, the tongue weight of the trailer pushes the rear end of the car down. The weight on the front wheels of the car is actually decreased, since the rear axle acts as a fulcrum. To exaggerate the point, if you pushed down hard enough on the extreme rear end of the car, the front wheels would lift off the ground and the rear wheels would support the entire weight of the car plus the tongue weight of the trailer. Actually, a good-sized trailer will make the front end of the tow car so light that it will weave at medium speeds, allowing the trailer to sway more readily, and diminishing the driver's control of the car. An equalizing hitch prevents that loss of control.

(2) The "equalizer" in an equalizing hitch is a lever attached to the ball mount, which, of course, is at the extreme

Hitches 29

rear of the tow car. If you lift the lever, it will lift the back of the car. If you lift it high enough, the back of the car will be just as high as it was before you put the trailer tongue on the ball.

(3) The end of the lever is provided with a chain that is pulled up and hooked onto the trailer beams. The higher you hook the chain, the higher you lift the back of the car (and the front of the trailer) and the more weight you shift to the front wheels. Some tongue weight is also shifted back to the trailer wheels.

To make it simple and easy to understand, Figure 3 shows just one lever. Actually, there are two. The two front trailer

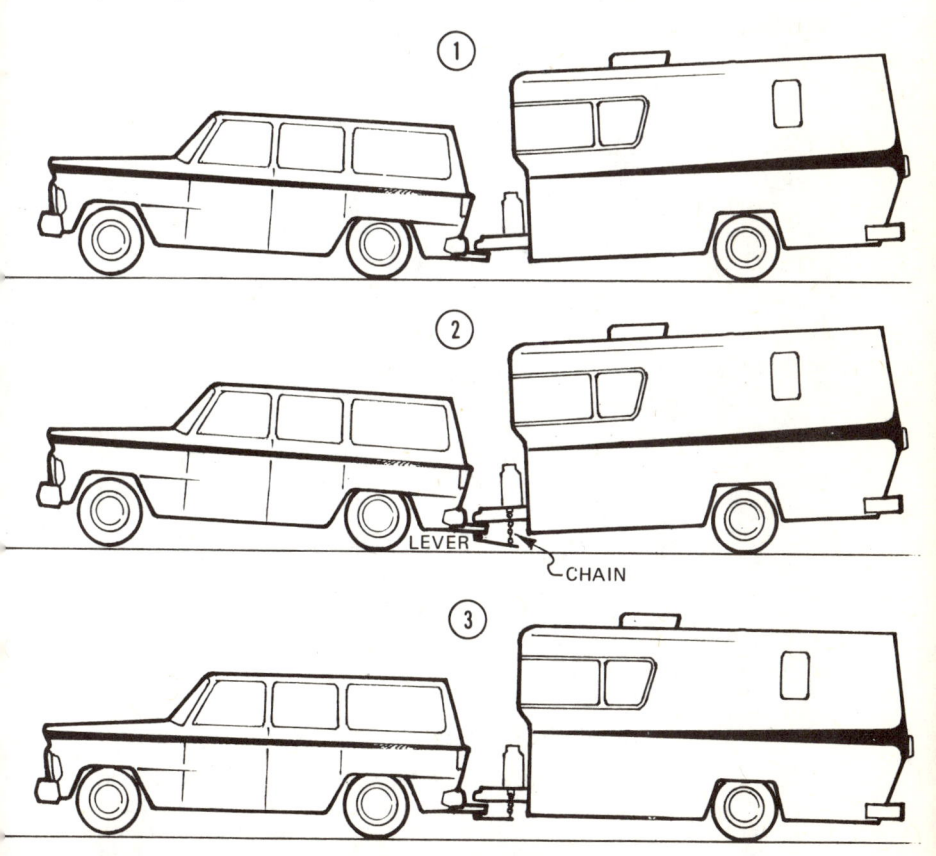

Fig. 3. Equalizing hitch

beams come together in a "V," and a lever is hooked on each side of the "V."

Different manufacturers attach the equalizing bars (levers) in different ways, but the principle is the same. The bars are in sockets so that they turn with the car. Turning moves one bar and chain forward and the other back a few inches.

Installing a Hitch

Your dealer will know welders who are experienced hitch installers, and *this is a job for experts*. The hitch can be bolted or welded to the car or both. Even if the hitch is to be bolted on, some welding will have to be done to attach the braces to the drawbar. Because every make and model of car and truck is different, each hitch has to be custom fitted.

Plate 5. Hitch installation: view under rear of our pickup truck. Metal painted a lighter color shows the hitch welded to braces and braces welded to truck frame. Electric socket is open. Hitch bar, with ball mount welded to it, slides into the square hole at right of photo and pin through hole holds it in place.

Some people prefer to have the hitch bolted on so that it can be easily removed when the car is traded in, and used on the new car. Bolting is perfectly satisfactory if it is properly done. But even if a hitch is welded on, it can be "burned" off with little trouble and used again. In either case, the hitch will have to be refitted.

As the sale of cars to be used as towing vehicles increases, manufacturers are paying more attention to optional towing equipment. They are now offering complete manufactured hitches that can be bolted onto some models. We are told that manufacturers prefer bolting to welding because there is a possibility that welding heat will weaken the frame. No doubt that is true. We have seen some really terrible welding jobs done by incompetent installers. On the other hand, a good, experienced hitch installer can make an excellent, safe welded hitch, but be sure you deal with an expert. If the car you are interested in offers a factory-made hitch, I know of no reason not to use a bolted-on hitch.

There are three methods of attaching a hitch to a tow vehicle: (1) attaching it to the bumper, (2) attaching it to the axle, or (3) attaching it to the frame. Only the third method is suitable for pulling a travel trailer. Attaching a hitch to bumper or axle might be suitable for pulling a light U-Haul trailer or light boat trailer, but for a travel trailer the bumper is not strong enough, and if you hook onto the axle you could easily damage it or pull out the whole rear end.

To install a frame hitch, the welder welds braces to a tow bar that extends several feet forward under the rear of the car, and then he welds the tow bar braces to the frame (Figure 4). Onto the rear of the tow bar he welds a square tube that sticks out beyond the rear of the car. The hitch bar to which the ball mount is attached slips into the square tube and is secured by inserting a short, heavy pull-pin through holes in the tube and hitch bar. The ball mount is welded onto the hitch bar at the correct height for your trailer and at a slight angle. The downward angle allows the equalizing bars (or spring bars), which attach to the ball mount, to slant downward. The bars must slant downward just a little so

32   TRAILERING

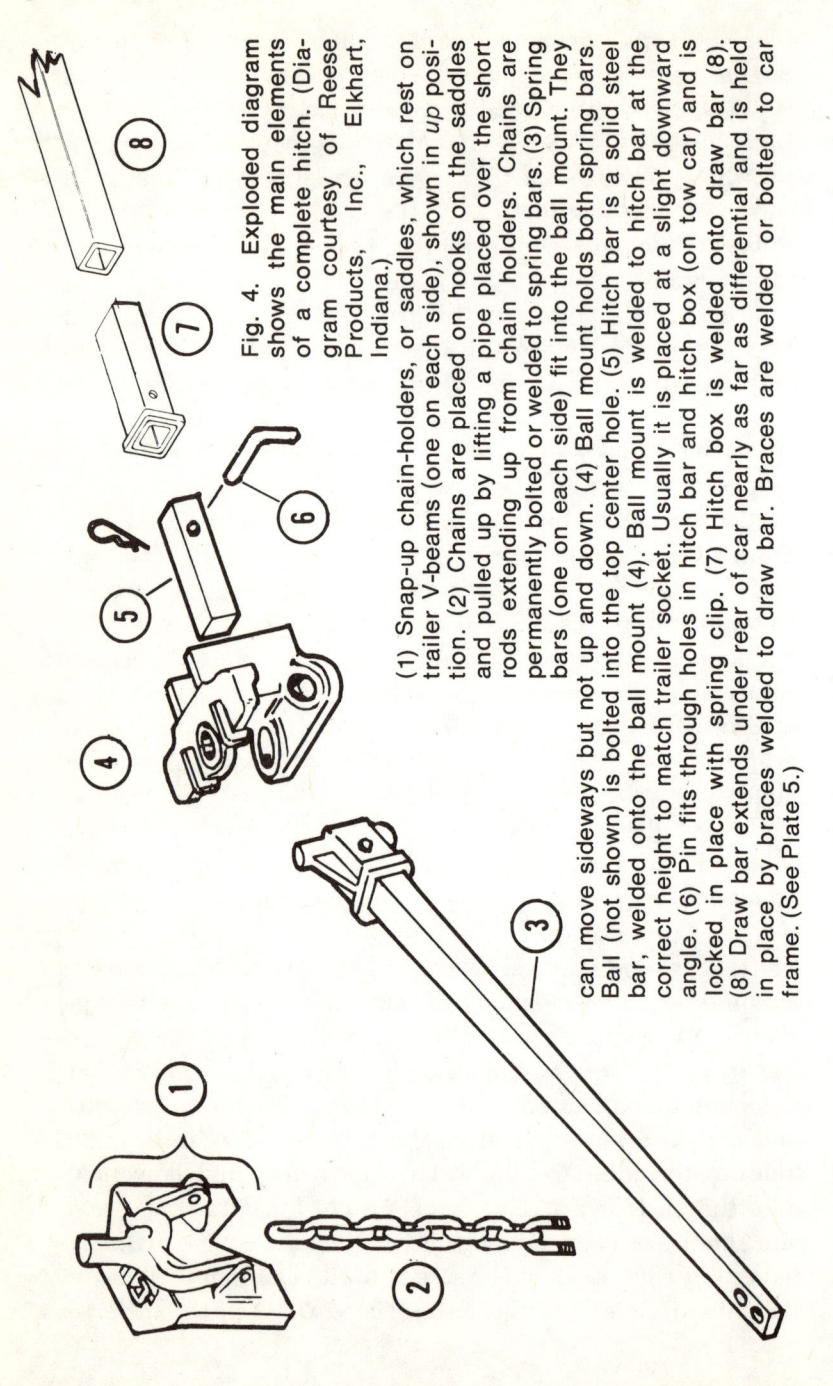

Fig. 4. Exploded diagram shows the main elements of a complete hitch. (Diagram courtesy of Reese Products, Inc., Elkhart, Indiana.)

(1) Snap-up chain-holders, or saddles, which rest on trailer V-beams (one on each side), shown in *up* position. (2) Chains are placed on hooks on the saddles and pulled up by lifting a pipe placed over the short rods extending up from chain holders. Chains are permanently bolted or welded to spring bars. (3) Spring bars (one on each side) fit into the ball mount. They can move sideways but not up and down. (4) Ball mount holds both spring bars. Ball (not shown) is bolted into the top center hole. (5) Hitch bar is a solid steel bar, welded onto the ball mount (4). Ball mount is welded to hitch bar at the correct height to match trailer socket. Usually it is placed at a slight downward angle. (6) Pin fits through holes in hitch bar and hitch box (on tow car) and is locked in place with spring clip. (7) Hitch box is welded onto draw bar (8). (8) Draw bar extends under rear of car nearly as far as differential and is held in place by braces welded to draw bar. Braces are welded or bolted to car frame. (See Plate 5.)

that they can be pulled up to raise the back of the car.

The height of the trailer hitch is not standard. When the trailer is perfectly level, the top of the ball should be about the same height as the trailer socket or perhaps an inch higher to allow for a little sag. When you put the trailer socket on the ball, the back of the car will sink, but when you pull up the chains on the spring bars, you will pull the car and trailer up to level again.

If the hitch is properly installed, when you pull the chains up until the car and trailer are level, the bars should bend a little. If they don't, they are not doing their job. As the trailer bounces on the road, the spring bars flex a bit along with the car's rear springs.

Hitches and equalizing bars are made in a number of sizes, or weights, depending on the weight they are designed to lift —from about 300 to 1,200 pounds. The heavier the tongue weight of the trailer and the weaker the springs of the tow car, the heavier the hitch that will be needed. Even with the equalizing hitch many passenger cars with soft springs will also require air lifts or helper springs.

It is a good idea to get a heavier hitch than you think you will need—for two reasons. One is that the tongue weight of the trailer is probably going to be a good deal heavier than you think. The other is that there is a good chance that you will want a larger trailer later on, when you get used to the small one.

The manufacturer of our first trailer said the tongue weight was 400 pounds. On the scales, it was 650. According to the dealer who sold us our second trailer, the tongue weight was supposed to be 600 pounds, but he said we had better allow for 700. On the scales, it was 1,100. I suppose the discrepancy exists because the manufacturer weighs it before the battery, propane tanks, and all other extras are put on and, of course, before the trailer is loaded. Some people carry a spare tire on the front "V" of the trailer, which adds to the weight.

Another hitch consideration is road clearance. Some ball mounts are made so that the spring bars extend back from the center of the mount. Others are attached through the bottom of the ball mount (Figure 5).

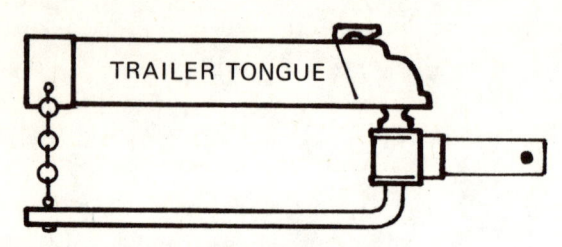

SPRING BARS FIT INTO BOTTOM OF BALL MOUNT — SO THEY ARE CLOSER TO GROUND.

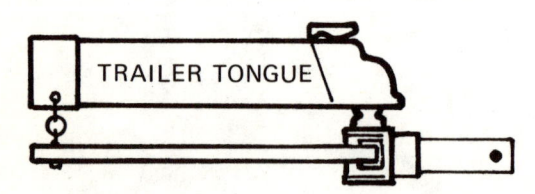

SPRING BARS FIT INTO CENTER OF BALL MOUNT — SO THEY ARE HIGHER OFF THE GROUND.

Fig. 5. Ball mounts

If you are towing a trailer that is quite low, it would probably be better to get a hitch with the equalizing bars attached in the center of the mount, so as to give you a couple more inches of road clearance. Our first trailer was quite low, and we banged the hitch on the ground any number of times, usually coming out of driveways. One time the bump was so hard that it cracked the ball mount, and we had to have it welded.

Once you have a good, strong hitch, you still need a few things to complete the hookup: sway control bar, safety chains, breakaway switch, and wiring.

Sway Control

Any conventional trailer has a tendency to sway in a crosswind, on bad roads, or when a large truck passes at high speed in the same direction the trailer is traveling (Figure 6). The largest surface of the car-trailer combination is between the rear wheels of the car and the trailer wheels. Therefore, wind pressure will be exerted most in that area causing the car to turn *toward* the direction of the pressure. Because the car turns toward the air pressure, this kind of sway, when caused by a passing truck, is often referred to as being "sucked in." We know of several trailers that were wrecked by being "sucked in" to passing trucks.

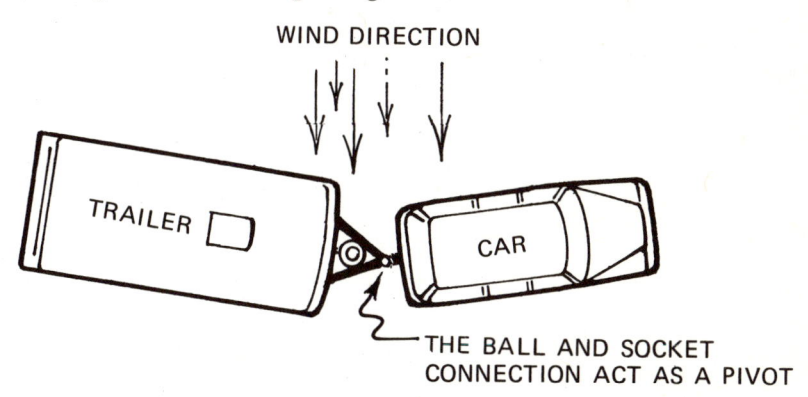

Fig. 6 Sway caused by passing truck

Longer trailers will obviously receive more pressure than short ones. In many cases, the tendency to sway will be greatly increased by loading the trailer too heavily in the rear. If you load a lot of heavy gear in the trailer trunk and inside the back of the trailer, the trailer tongue and the back wheels of the car will be too light. The heavy weight in the back of the trailer will swing the trailer back and forth like a pendulum, a dangerous situation even at medium speeds and a very dangerous situation at high speeds. It is better to have a little too much tongue weight than too little. Too much tongue weight is dangerous only if it overloads your car's suspension and tires (especially tires) or if the weight is more than the equalizing bars can handle. The ideal tongue weight is said to be 15 percent of the trailer's total weight. If your loaded trailer weighs 4,000 pounds, the tongue weight should be 600 pounds.

Swaying can be controlled very well with a device that resists the wind pressure and makes the car-trailer combination hard to "bend" at the pivot. Probably the most common method of reducing sway is to place a friction brake between car and trailer (Figure 7).

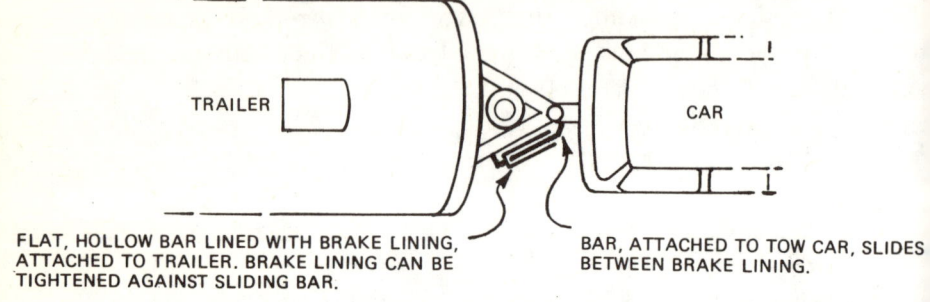

FLAT, HOLLOW BAR LINED WITH BRAKE LINING, ATTACHED TO TRAILER. BRAKE LINING CAN BE TIGHTENED AGAINST SLIDING BAR.

BAR, ATTACHED TO TOW CAR, SLIDES BETWEEN BRAKE LINING.

Fig. 7. Friction brake

Another popular method of controlling sway is a set of cams at the ends of both spring bars (Figure 8). As the car turns, the upper movable cams are forced upward onto the lower fixed cams; and the upper cams, trying to slide back down into their original position, tend to push the trailer back into a straight line with the car. At the same time, as the cams push up toward the top position, the back of the car is raised a little, which transfers more weight to the car's front wheels. All very good.

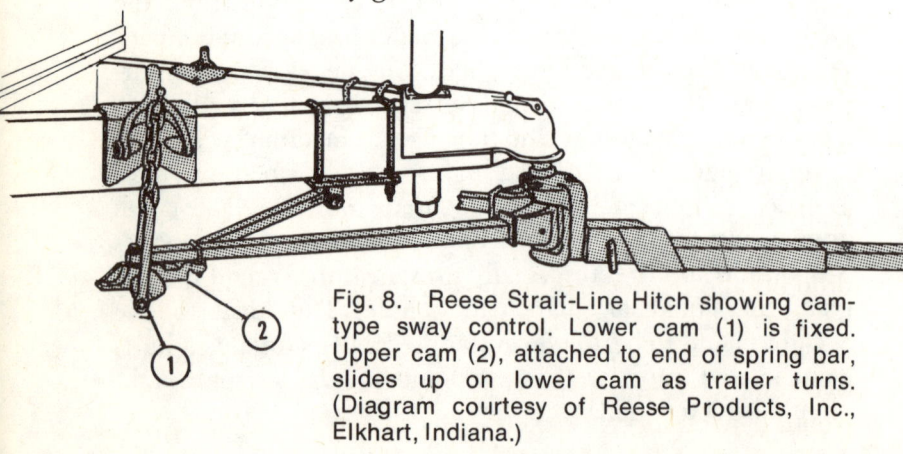

Fig. 8. Reese Strait-Line Hitch showing cam-type sway control. Lower cam (1) is fixed. Upper cam (2), attached to end of spring bar, slides up on lower cam as trailer turns. (Diagram courtesy of Reese Products, Inc., Elkhart, Indiana.)

We have talked with many trailerites who prefer the cams, but having used both kinds, we prefer the friction brake. We feel that there is a slight lag in the cam action that allows some sway to start before the cams fully respond to the turn. On the other hand, the friction bar holds a tight rein at all times. It might be a good idea to use both at the same time; there's no reason why you shouldn't.

There are other methods, but whatever they are, the principle is to resist the turning pressure. Even with the sway bars (which should be called "anti-sway" bars), when a big truck passes you at high speed in the same direction, you will still feel a tug on the steering wheel. But it should be slight.

Uneven roads can cause sway, too, but if they are very bad, you probably will have slowed down to a speed at which the sway won't matter. Whatever the cause, sway bars will control the sway.

Safety Chains

Many states require safety chains to keep the trailer connected to the tow car even if the hitch should fall off. It has happened, as a result of bad welds or sheared bolts. Even if you live in a state that does not require safety chains, you might consider having them put on, because you will probably be traveling in states that do require them. New York State, where we bought our second trailer, does not require them, and when we came to the Pennsylvania Turnpike toll booth, the attendant said we couldn't enter—no safety chain. However, after some discussion and a thorough inspection, he decided that the rest of our hitch was so rugged that he would let us go on.

There is some controversy as to whether safety chains are really desirable. Many people feel that it is more dangerous to have a trailer dangling at the end of a chain than to let it drop off and be stopped by the trailer brakes—which would be actuated by the break-away switch.

I am no expert on the subject, and I doubt if any comparative tests have ever been made, but I should think that it would depend a great deal on how the safety chains are installed. California law on the subject seems sensible. It requires that short chains be welded to the tongue of the trailer and attached by strong hooks to the car. The chains should be short, so that they would hold the trailer tongue off the ground if the hitch failed.

You can buy a safety chain at trailer stores. In the center of the chain there is a loop that fits over the jack post. The two ends then go down between the beams in the "V" and up on either side of the jack post, where each chain is fastened by a hook to the car. This method also would keep the trailer off the ground, assuming the chain and hooks were strong enough and of the correct length (Plate 6).

Plate 6. Safety chain, purchased from trailer store, is long enough to allow trailer to turn, but short enough to hold trailer tongue off the ground. Note middle of chain looped around jack post.

Break-Away Switch

The break-away switch is another safety device required by law almost everywhere, on all trailers large enough to require brakes (Plate 7). Of course, the switch will only work on trailers equipped with electric brakes. The positive pole of the trailer battery is connected to one lead from the break-away switch, and the other lead from the switch is connected

Hitches 39

to wire that goes to the brakes. If the plunger in the switch is pulled out, contact is made inside the switch, and the battery current flows to the brakes (Figure 9). If the trailer should come unhooked from the tow car, the plunger would be pulled out of the switch, making contact, causing electricity to flow to the brakes, and stopping the runaway trailer.

Plate 7. Break-away switch. Wires entering on the left go to battery and trailer brakes. Wire to right from the plunger is hooked to tow car. When plunger is pulled out, brakes are actuated.

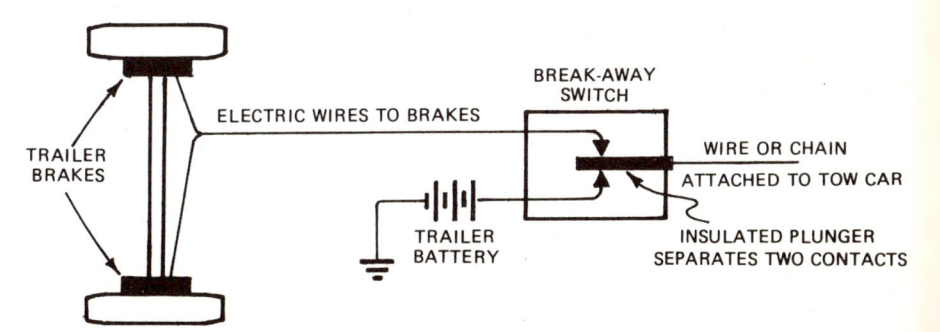

Fig. 9. Wiring of break-away switch

Fifth Wheelers

The so-called fifth-wheel trailer is designed to hook into a socket that is secured into the back of a pickup truck (Plate 8). All the tongue weight of the trailer is on or slightly in front of the rear axle. This arrangement has several advantages:

Plate 8. Twenty-seven-foot fifth wheeler hooked up and ready to go. Note that you can tow a considerably longer trailer without increasing overall length. (Photo courtesy of Hyland Mfg. Co., Carlisle, Iowa.)

(1) Since the "pivot" is over the rear axle, sway is practically eliminated.

(2) You can make a sharper turn.

(3) Hooking and unhooking is easier. No safety chains, equalizing hitches, or sway bars are necessary.

(4) You can pull a considerably longer trailer without increasing the overall length of your rig.

But the fifth wheeler has a number of disadvantages:

(1) Many trailerites prefer a passenger car as a tow car, not a pickup truck.

(2) There is little space in the tow pickup for gear, and what space there is, is exposed to the weather. Most people who use pickups to pull their trailers have caps over the truck bed, where they carry all kinds of traveling paraphernalia. If you have a fifth wheeler, you have to carry almost everything inside the trailer.

(3) Since many camper cabs and pickups have bunks in them, they can be used for short side trips on roads where it

Hitches 41

would not be practical to pull a trailer. You couldn't do that with a fifth wheeler.

(4) Practically all the tongue weight is on the rear tires, and there is no way to transfer any weight forward. That need not be a disadvantage if you make sure you have enough tires to carry the weight.

(5) The bedroom is in the front over the truck. It is much roomier than the bed in a camper over the cab; but unless you are very short, you can't stand up. There are stairs leading up to the bedroom, but you have to bend over when you get up there. This wouldn't be bad on a vacation trip, but I don't know if I would want to do it for long periods—if, like ourselves, you want to be full-time trailerites.

(6) We have heard some objection to the odd appearance of the fifth wheeler when it is parked without the pickup (Plate 9).

Plate 9. Fifth wheeler parked in a trailer park

By all means look them over and see for yourself whether the advantages or the disadvantages are more important to you.

A very recent development is the car-top hitch, the fifth-wheeler idea applied to passenger cars. A steel plate is mounted on the car top and the socket is attached to the plate. As Plate 10 shows, the car can turn completely around

Plate 10. A recent development—fifth wheeler designed to be towed by a passenger car, instead of a truck. (Photo courtesy of Harmon Industries, Warrensburg, Missouri.)

and push the trailer into tight places. At the present writing, only one company is manufacturing this type of trailer, and production is still very limited.

6

Wiring

THERE ARE AS many as seven wiring connections between the car and the trailer (Figure 10): (1) running lights, (2) right turn and stop signal, (3) left turn and stop signal, (4) hot line to charge battery, (5) brakes, (6) ground, and (7) back-up lights, if your trailer has them.

Brakes

The brake connection is the only one that is slightly complicated. When you step on the brake pedal, you don't want the trailer brakes to grab full-force and lock the wheels. You want them to act the way the car brakes do. When you touch the brake pedal lightly, you want the brakes to slow the trailer, and as you push harder on the pedal, you want the breaking power to increase.

To control the trailer brakes, a variable rheostat (called a *brake controller*) is connected in the wire to the brakes. This rheostat is actuated by the same brake fluid that operates the car's brakes. There is also a hand control lever, so that the

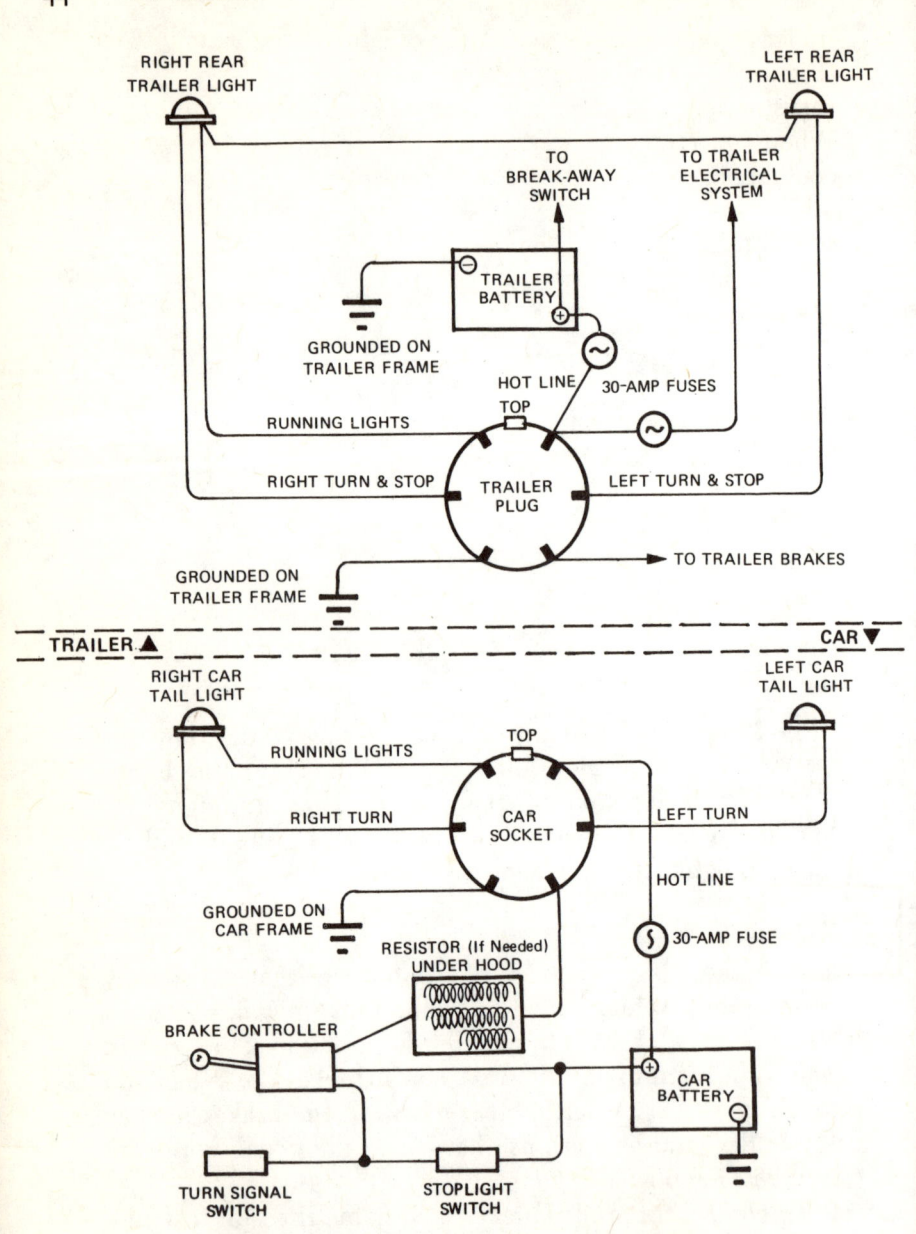

SIMPLIFIED DIAGRAM OF CAR TO TRAILER WIRING
Refer to this Diagram as you Read This Section on Wiring.

Fig. 10

Wiring 45

trailer brakes can be used independently of the car brakes (Figure 11). The battery current increases as you move the rheostat lever to the right, and braking power increases. When you take your foot off the pedal, a spring pushes the contact off the rheostat and no current flows.

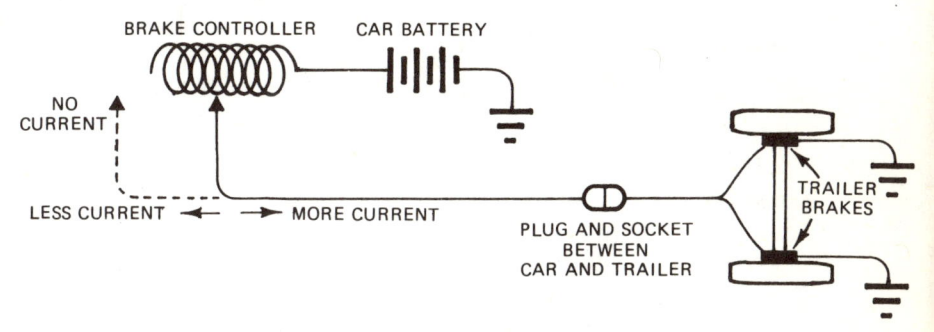

Fig. 11. Brake controller

The tubing that holds the brake fluid does not have to be cut when you install the brake controller. At the point where the tubing leaves the master cylinder or power brake distribution block, the tubing can be disconnected and a "T" installed. "Ts" are furnished with the controller kit. Then the brake tubing is replaced in the one branch of the "T" and the tubing from the brake controller goes in the other (Figure 12).

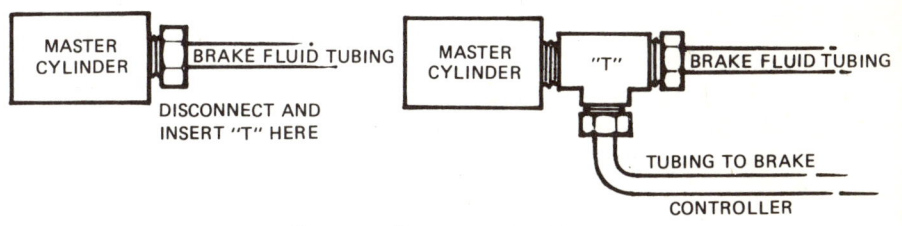

Fig. 12. Brake fluid tubing

When you push the brake pedal, the brake fluid pushes a plunger in the brake controller, so that it moves a contact across the rheostat. When you first start pushing the pedal, the entire resistance of the rheostat coil is in the circuit to the trailer brakes (Figure 13). As you increase the brake pres-

46 TRAILERING

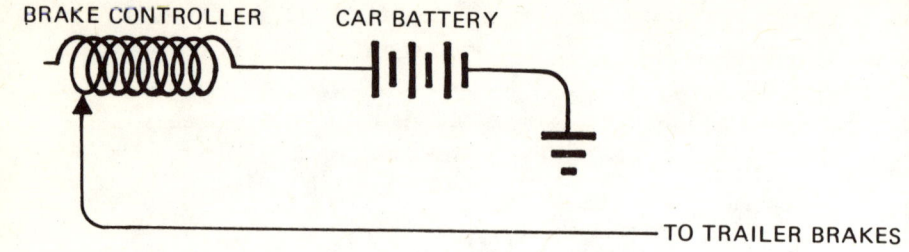

Fig. 13. More resistance

sure, the electrical contact moves across the rheostat (an electrical resistance coil) so that there is less and less resistance until, when the brake pedal is all the way down, the battery is connected to the brake wire with no resistance, and the full current of the battery is flowing to the trailer brake-magnet coils (Figure 14).

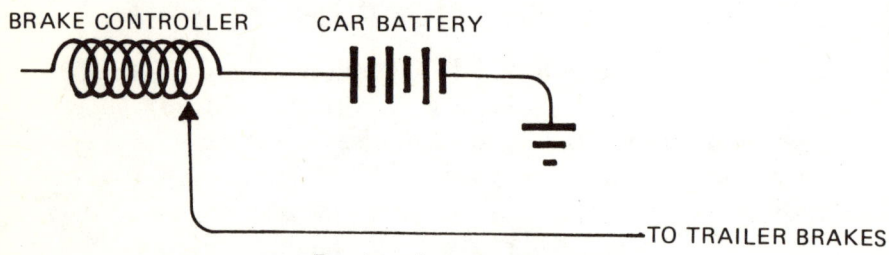

Fig. 14. Less resistance

The brake controller is mounted just under the dash or on the steering column, where the driver can reach the brake controller handle quickly.

There are many times when you will want to operate the trailer brakes but not the car brakes, particularly on slippery roads, going downhill, or on curves. By applying the trailer brakes *only*, you can prevent the car and trailer from jackknifing. On most controllers you can adjust the rheostat so that the trailer brakes begin to take hold just slightly before the car brakes. That is the way they should be adjusted, as a precaution against jackknifing.

On light trailers or trailers with two-wheel brakes (instead of four), you will probably need an additional permanent resistance in the brake line. If too much electricity reaches the brake magnets, they will "grab," and you won't get a smooth stop. One popular resistor has three fixed resistances, with terminals so arranged that you can connect to a very short resistance, to several longer lengths, or to the whole thing (Figure 15). There is also a circular resistor with a movable contact like a clock hand (Figure 16). Either kind works well. Before you can tell just how much resistance you need, you will have to take the trailer out on the road and try the brakes. If they grab, use progressively more resistance until the grabbing stops.

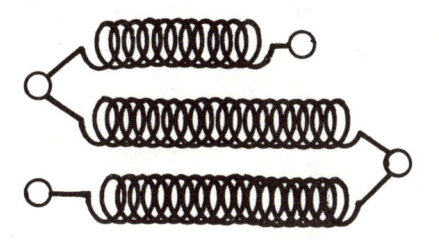

Fig. 15.   Resistor

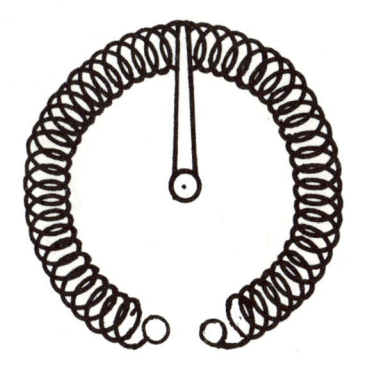

Fig. 16.   Circular resistor

Any resistor will heat up if enough current flows through it long enough. The resistance inside a brake controller will heat it up if you keep your foot on the brake pedal too long, and eventually it will start to smoke. So, if you stop for

48 TRAILERING

longer than the average traffic light, take your foot off the brake pedal and shift into "park."

There is one additional electrical connection for the trailer brakes. To hook up a third lead from the brake controller to the stoplight switch so that the trailer stoplights will go on when you use the manual control only, connect the third controller wire to the wire from the turn-signal switch in the tow car (Figure 17).

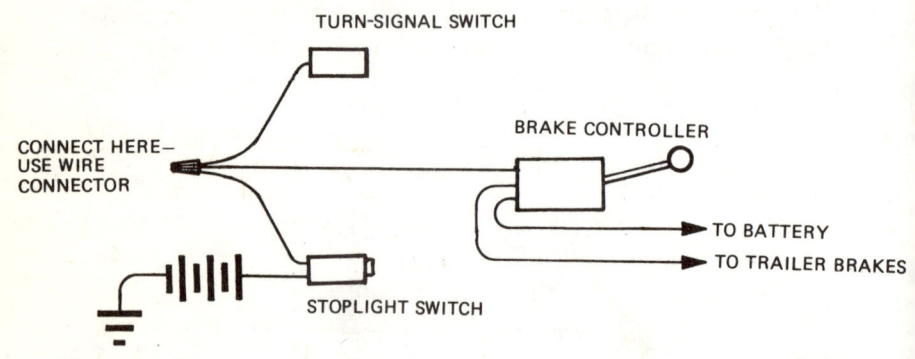

Fig. 17. Connections between trailer brakes and trailer stoplights

Figure 18 shows the wiring for electric brakes in greater detail.

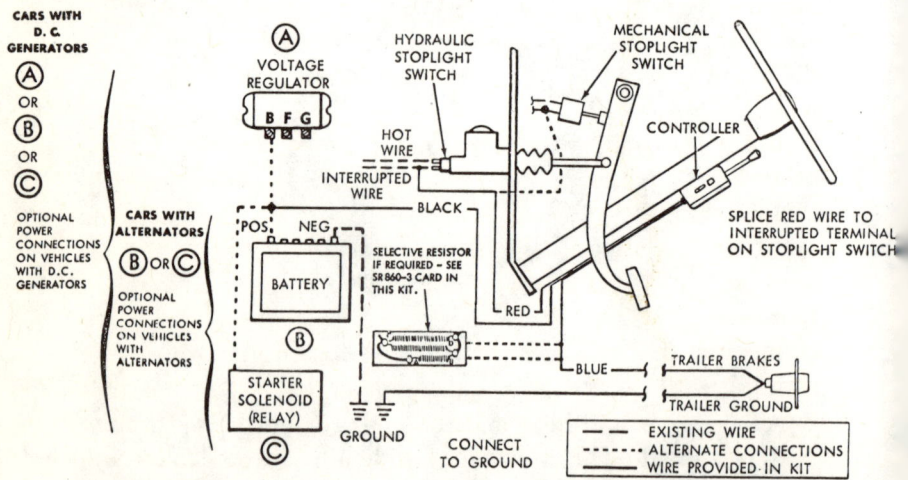

Fig. 18. Wiring diagram for electric brakes. (Courtesy of Kelsey Hayes Company, Romulus, Michigan.)

Hydraulic Brakes

A few trailers have hydraulic brakes, like those in the tow car. In this case, a flexible hose is connected to the car's hydraulic tubing system. A connector joins the car's tubing to the trailer's, but the connection is mechanical. Brake fluid does not flow between car and trailer. So, when you step on the brake pedal, all brakes on car and trailer work at the same time.

There is another kind of hydraulic brake system for trailers called *surge brakes*, which have no hydraulic connector between the car and trailer. When you step on the brake pedal to stop the car, the inertia of the trailer pushing toward the car actuates a plunger in the trailer brake system.

Since I have no firsthand experience with either of these systems, all I can do is tell you that they are available. One cautious trailering friend had his tandem-axle trailer made with hydraulic brakes on one axle and electric brakes on the other, so in case one system failed, the other would still work.

Lights

The running lights and the right- and left-turn lights (and backup lights if you have them) can be connected easily by attaching wires from the car's rear trailer-connector socket to the wires that go to the rear lights of the car. To find out which wire is which, use a 12-volt test light. Ground one lead from the test light to the car chassis. Using a needle on the other lead, stick it thru the insulation on the wires going to the rear lights. As you test each wire, turn on the car lights and then the left- and right-turn signals. When the test light goes on, you know you have the correct lead. Then connect that wire from the socket permanently. You can purchase connectors that connect through the insulation, or you can skin the wire for a short distance, make the connection, and tape it.

If you don't have a diagram showing which connection goes to which terminal in the rear socket, the easiest way to find out is to plug the trailer plug into the car socket and, with a separate wire, connect the trailer chassis to the car chassis to make a temporary ground connection. Then touch each of the car-light leads, which you have already identified, to each of the socket wires, until the corresponding trailer light goes on. In other words, when you turn on the car lights, touch each of the socket wires until the trailer lights go on. Then the right turn, then the left turn. Then have a helper listen to the trailer brakes while you touch the brake lead from the controller to the remaining socket terminals. When the brake magnets click, that's the correct terminal. Now make a permanent ground connection on your car and remove the temporary ground connection. With the car lights turned on, touch the permanent ground lead to the remaining unused socket wires. When the trailer running lights go on, that's the terminal for the ground connection.

That leaves only one connection, the "hot" lead to charge your battery. This connection is a wire from the car battery to the trailer battery, fused at both ends. Positive connection to positive connection. In practice, the wire to your car battery can be connected to the starter solenoid, or the battery connection to the voltage regulator. Wires from these connections go directly to the battery positive terminal, so it is exactly the same as connecting directly to the battery. The only reason for connecting to one or the other is convenience. Make whichever connection is easier.

Near each battery, at both ends of the hot line, put a 30-ampere fuse. An easy way to install the fuse is to get in-line fuse holders for 30-ampere fuses at an auto store, cut the wire leads near each battery, and connect the wires from the fuse holders to the cut ends.

Most of the trailerites we have talked with have the impression that this charge line will keep their trailer battery charged just the same as their car battery, but that isn't exactly true. If your car battery is low and you hook up the electrical connection to your trailer, the car alternator (or generator) will charge both batteries at equal rates until the car battery is fully charged. Then the voltage regulator in your car will reduce the charge to practically zero. If you leave the car and trailer connected because your trailer battery is still low, the car battery will "drain" into the trailer battery until both batteries are equally charged. But that is a very slow process; the battery will not be charged nearly so fast as it is when the alternator is doing the charging. A good analogy is drawing water from a full tank to an empty one (Figure 19). If the connecting pipe (wire) is large, it will drain faster. If a pump (alternator) is put in the line, it will fill the empty tank much faster.

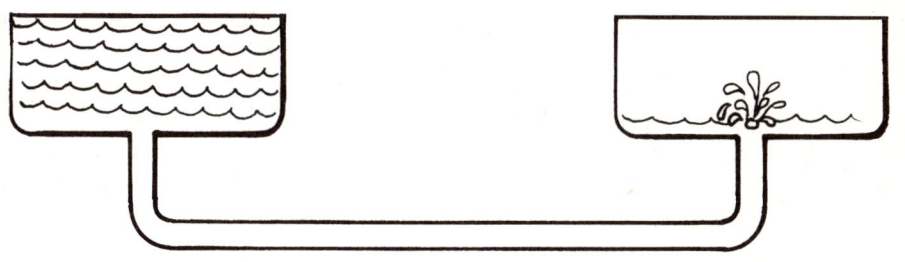

Fig. 19. A car battery will "drain" into a trailer battery until both are equally charged.

You can buy an electronic device that will automatically switch the alternator to charge whichever battery needs it most. If you use a lot of electricity when you go camping, this is a good thing to have. However, we have a slightly different system and have never found it necessary.

What we do is connect the car and trailer batteries with heavy cable whenever we are going to be in the boondocks for an extended time, and we leave them connected. When we take the car to go shopping or sightseeing, we disconnect the cable from the car battery; but as soon as we return to the trailer, we connect them again. Since we are using our car every day or two or three, the car battery is always well charged, and that in turn charges the trailer battery. With both batteries always connected, the amount of charge used up in either battery is only half what it would be if only the trailer battery were being used. The possible danger of this method is that you might discharge your car battery to the point where it would not start your car. We have never had this happen, but it is possible if you don't use the car enough to keep the battery charged.

We have been on batteries only for as long as six weeks and never had the slightest trouble. And we use a good bit of electricity. In addition to our lights and air compressor for the water tank, we have the inverter, which produces 110 volts for the sewing machine, typewriter, ¼-inch drill, TV, hair clippers, and hand mixer. Friends have used this system for five months at a time with no difficulty.

The mechanics of the system are very simple. You could simply plug the trailer electric plug into the car socket, and that would connect the two batteries. But we use a separate electric cable for two reasons: (1) We may not want to position the car so that it is directly in front of the trailer where we could plug it in, and (2) by using a heavy cable to connect the two batteries, the charging process is speeded up.

Use no. 10 flexible cable if you can find it. The electrical stores where we were located at the time didn't carry it, so we obtained 60 feet of no. 12 flexible two-wire cable and cut it in half. Then we connected the two wires in each cable and used one length for the positive connection and one for the negative connection. We put a permanent grounded receptacle under the trailer battery, connected it to the trailer battery, connected a grounded socket to the car battery, and, finally, connected grounded plugs to each end of the 30-foot cable (Figure 20).

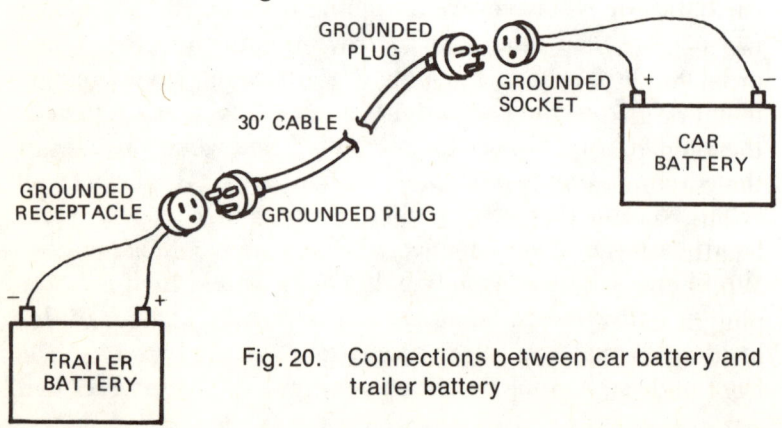

Fig. 20. Connections between car battery and trailer battery

The only reason for using the grounded plugs and sockets is that the polarity cannot be reversed. The ground connection is not used. Positive is always connected to positive, and negative to negative. If you were to connect positive to negative, both batteries would be discharged very quickly, and the connecting wire would heat up.

When you are making the connections, you can easily check them by making all the positive connections on the gold-colored terminals and all the negative connections on the silver-colored terminals. A final test: When you are ready to plug in the plug to the car socket (having already connected the trailer battery end), push it in and pull it out quickly. If it sparks, you have some connection wrong. If it doesn't spark, the connections are right. If you have a converter, disconnect the negative lead from the trailer battery to the trailer while you are testing. Sparking wires can harm the converter.

When the two batteries are connected, the thinner the wire, the greater the resistance and the greater the voltage drop. Twelve-volt battery current needs very large wire or the voltage drop becomes serious. So, if you use two no. 12 wires as one wire, you have approximately the equivalent of no. 9 wire, which is very heavy but none too heavy for the 12-volt DC. The heavier the wire, the better.

One last suggestion: Attach a short piece of rubber garden hose (about two inches long) by a string to the cable near the car battery plug. When you disconnect this plug in order to use your car, slip the hose over the prongs of the plug in order to prevent the prongs from accidentally touching any metal on the trailer and shorting your trailer battery; or slip the plug prongs into a dummy electrical socket. Then coil the wire up under the trailer so that it is protected from rain.

The socket is attached to the car battery with short lengths of heavy wire and left hanging from the battery. When you return to the trailer in your car, open the hood, plug in the cable plug from the trailer battery, and close the hood again. There is plenty of room to lead the cable out the front under the hood.

# 7

Towing Vehicles

We have seen just about every kind of car or truck pulling nearly every kind of trailer. Frankly, we wouldn't want to ride in some of them.

Our own feeling is that we don't want to take any more chances than we have to. We want every kind of equipment on our car (or truck) and trailer that will add to safety. Why not keep the odds in our favor? Besides that, we don't want the nuisance of having a breakdown on the road or in some out-of-the-way place.

But you will find many different opinions about the kind of car and the kind of equipment you need. Of course, what you need will vary with the size and weight of the trailer, the distance to be traveled, and the type of roads and grades you expect to encounter. If you are going to pull a small, light trailer, your equipment doesn't matter too much. As the size and weight of the trailer gets larger, however, it becomes more and more important to have the right kind of tow vehicle with the right kind of equipment.

All car manufacturers today offer a towing package that

consists of a larger radiator, six-blade fan with shroud, larger battery, larger alternator, and sometimes special wiring to make it easy to connect the lights to your rear socket. You also get heavier rear springs. A trailer package is comparatively inexpensive if you order it when you order a new car, but it would cost a lot if you added these extras later. So if you are going to buy a new car, by all means order the trailer package. And if you are going to get a manually-operated transmission, be sure that it is heavy duty.

Transmission Coolers

If you buy a car with an automatic transmission, another thing to consider, especially if you have a fairly heavy trailer, is an additional transmission cooler. Most cars use a separate section of the radiator to cool the transmission fluid. In hot weather, if you are running on steep grades—especially with the wind against you—the transmission oil is likely to get quite hot. Since the most frequent cause of transmission failure is overheating, an additional transmission cooler is a very worthwhile device.

Transmission coolers come in different sizes. If you get a big one, completely disconnect your transmission oil lines from your radiator and hook them to the new transmission cooler. Or you can put the cooler in the return line so that the oil flows through the radiator first and then through the separate cooler and back to the transmission.

We have no heating problem with our truck, so we use the latter method. But if your car has a tendency to heat up, it would be better to use the separate cooler only. Instructions for connecting the cooler come with the kit. I have installed them on two cars, following instructions, and found it rather a simple job.

Another device you might consider is an electric fuel pump—not to replace your regular pump, but strictly as an auxiliary. During hot weather, excessive engine heat can vaporize gasoline in the fuel line before it gets to the carburetor, blocking the flow of gasoline and causing the engine to stall (vapor lock). You can have a small electric pump installed in the fuel line. The pump will run on a 12-volt current from the battery. If you feel a vapor lock developing, flip on the toggle switch on the dashboard to operate the electric pump, which will force the gasoline on through the fuel line.

Rear-End Ratio

When you order a car with a trailer package, you will also get a lower rear-end gear ratio. In simple terms, this means that if the ratio is 3, the drive shaft turns around three times to make the wheel turn one revolution. The higher the ratio number, the more power is delivered to the wheel, and, of course, the faster the engine turns to maintain the same speed. If you pull a heavy trailer, you need a higher rear-end gear ratio than if you pull a smaller one. Also, if you have a low-powered engine, you need a higher gear ratio than you need with a high-powered engine. The mathematics of this is complicated and beyond me; but automobile and truck companies publish data and tables showing their recommendations. You may not notice much difference on level ground, but when you get on steep grades, you will need the higher gear ratio. Actual gear ratios are usually expressed in decimal figures, such as 2.73 or 3.56. Our pickup truck has a 4.10 rear end, which enables us to pull a heavy trailer.

One caution—most car salesmen know less about pulling a trailer than you do, so it would be a good idea to find someone experienced in trailering to help you with specifications before you sign on the dotted line.

Tires

Another thing to be sure of is tires. We had a blowout once because we had a lot more tongue weight than we thought we had, and the 6-ply tires were overloaded. The next time we bought 8-ply tires, and now we have 10-plys. You need the heavy tires more on the back than on the front, but we put them all around so that we could rotate the tires and keep the wear approximately even. If you load up your trunk, as most people do when they travel, you are likely to need heavier-duty tires than you might think. Add the weight of the trunk load and the tongue weight and then consult a tire dealer's tire chart. The chart will tell you how much weight each size and grade of tire will safely support. One additional bit of advice—before you start out on a trip, check the lugs on both car and trailer, to be sure they are good and tight. And be sure to have sufficient air pressure in your tires.

The equalizing hitch, you will recall, equalizes the amount of weight on each tire. Let's suppose you weigh the front and rear of your car so that you know the weight on the front and back wheels. When you hook on the trailer, you have a tongue weight of 900 pounds, and the equalizing hitch transfers 300 pounds to the front wheels. Although the scales show that weight distribution when the car is standing still, it will change continuously as you drive. At the bottom of a hill, as the car moves upward again, the weight on the front tires increases and the weight on the back tires decreases. But on top of a hill, the rear tires carry most of the weight. On a long slope, the difference is not great, but on a short slope like a driveway, the weight shift can be very great. So, even with the equalizing hitches, there are times when two tires will be carrying almost all of the extra tongue weight.

How Much Engine?

When we bought our first trailer, our tow car had a 304-cubic-inch engine, which was supposed to develop 190 gross horsepower. Actually, the net horsepower was less, because air conditioning, air pollution equipment, power steering, power brakes, and other equipment used up considerable power. Our new truck has a 400-cubic-inch engine and is much more satisfactory for pulling a 30-foot trailer.

The Airstream Company has a simple formula that will give you a good idea of how much power you will need:

$$\frac{\text{Trailer Weight} + \text{Car Weight}}{\text{Engine Horsepower}} = \text{Weight Each Horsepower Pulls}$$

Maximum amount each horsepower should pull is 60 pounds.

Between 30 and 40 pounds is adequate.

Use the nominal, or gross horsepower, in your calculations.

Larger engines use more gas, of course, but it would be poor economy to get an under-powered engine. If your engine is working to its limit all the time, you won't save much on gas, maybe nothing. You will spend a lot more on repair bills, and you won't enjoy creeping up a hill in low gear with a string of cars behind you waiting to pass.

8

Hooking Up

So now you have the right-sized trailer for your purpose, the hitch is on, and all the electrical connections are wired. You are ready to hook up and try it on the road.

Turn the jack-post handle to raise the front of the trailer high enough so that the ball on the back of the car will fit under it. Then raise the socket-locking lever (otherwise the socket won't fit down over the ball). Back up the car *slowly*, with someone standing next to the trailer tongue to signal left, right, and stop. With a little practice, you will find this procedure very easy. You can do it yourself without help, but you will probably have to get out and look a few times. Mirrors that fasten over the jack post are available at trailer stores. These enable you to see the socket from the driver's seat through the rear window.

When the hitch ball is directly over the socket, lower it onto the ball and close the locking lever. Secure the locking lever with a nut and bolt, with a special locking pin that you can buy, or with a padlock. We feel safer with a padlock. If you were to hit a bump or pothole, the trailer could jump off the hitch ball if it were not well secured. You would be surprised how easily screws and nuts can be loosened by vibration and come off.

Next, raise the trailer tongue again, as high as you can jack it without straining. Now you can put on the equalizing bars and pull them up, without having to lift the car and trailer too. Attach the bars and put the correct chain link on the hook (the correct link will hold the car and trailer level). If one link seems a trifle too high and the next one a trifle low, keep it on the higher link. The higher you put the chain, the more weight you lift off the rear wheels of the car. But the rear wheels must not be lifted *too* high. If there is insufficient weight on the drive wheel, it will spin under starting loads and on upgrades, causing the tire to wear out long before it should.

After the bars are on, lower the trailer all the way, so that the entire weight of the trailer is on the ball, and crank the jack post up out of the way for traveling. Check to see if car and trailer are level. If the hitch is too high or too low, jack it up again and try a higher or lower chain link; then lower the tongue again. When you get it just right, mark the link that goes on the hook with a daub of paint, a piece of tape, or wire, so that you can remember which link goes on the hook.

Attach the break-away wire to a part of the car or hitch that can't come off. The bumper is a good place.

Attach the safety chain to the tow car. If you don't have a good place to put the hooks on the end of the safety chain, it would be a good idea to have a welder attach a pair of heavy rings or knobs to your car. Any welding shop can do it at little cost.

Then connect your sway bar and tighten it snugly. Don't jam it or force it, but be sure it's snug. Try it out on the road to see how it performs when a fast truck goes by in the same direction you are going. If you get too much jolt, tighten it a little tighter until you feel only a slight tug on the steering wheel.

Finally, plug in the electric connector all the way. Most connector sockets have a spring-loaded lid that hooks down on the plug and keeps it from pulling out. Before you do anything else, have your partner stand in the back of the trailer and check to see if the lights, brakes, and turn signals are working. Step on the brake pedal—brake lights on? Push the brake controller lever over—brake lights on again? Check the turn signals both ways. You can check the brakes by having someone stand next to the trailer wheels. While you step on the brake pedal, have your partner listen for the click of the brake magnets. Then, as soon as you start moving, push the brake controller lever to see if the trailer brakes alone will stop you.

The description of hooking up makes it sound like a long job. Actually, it takes only a few minutes. It's like trying to tell you in words how to tie your shoelace. It takes a long, complicated description to tell you how to do something you do in seconds and hardly think about.

After you are all hooked up and ready to go *check everything*. Once, when I was in a hurry, I started off with the jack post down. Another time, I left behind a tool box and didn't know it until the next day. It took a lot of long distance phoning and expense to get it back.

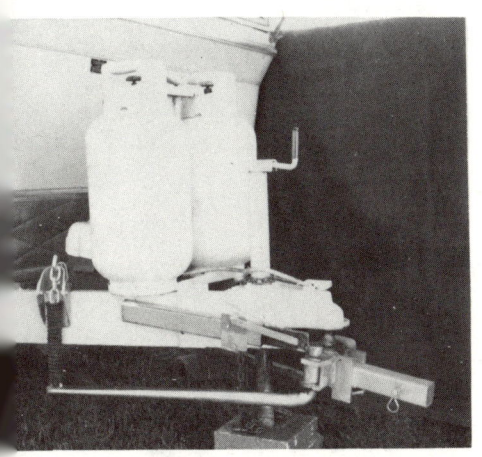

Plate 11. Left, when the trailer is parked, a convenient way to store the ball mount and equalizing bars is to put them back on the trailer. Plate 12. When you are ready to hook up again, right, remove the equalizing bars.

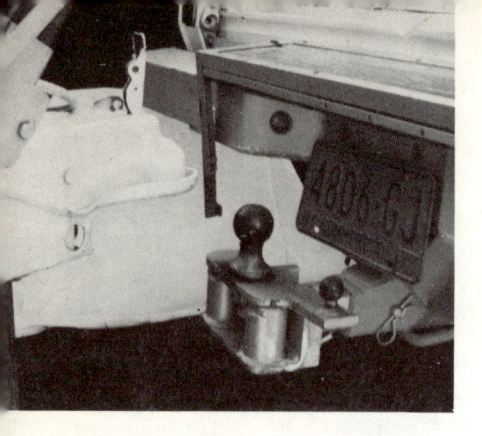

Plate 13. Transfer ball mount to truck, push in the pin, and secure it with spring clip.

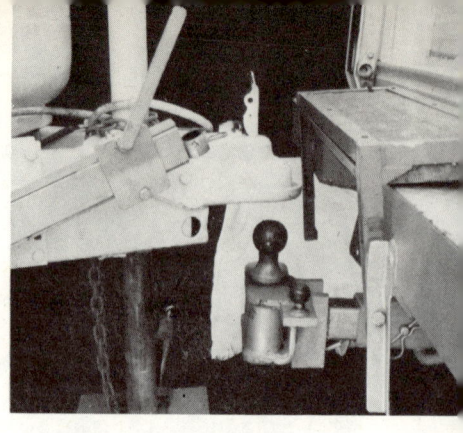

Plate 14. Back truck until ball is directly under socket.

Plate 17. Put equalizing bars in place.

Plate 18. Hang chain on hook, using the proper chain link, and jack up tongue as high as you can without straining.

Plate 19. Put steel rod in place in chain holder.

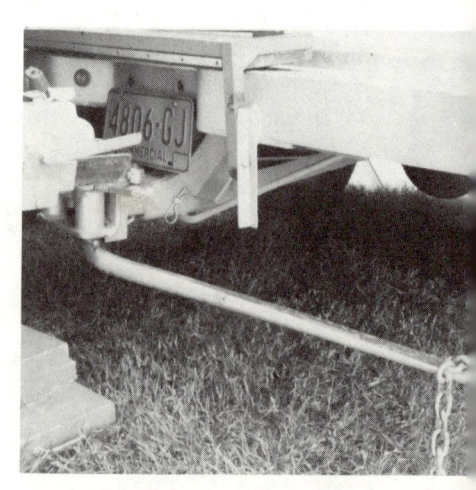

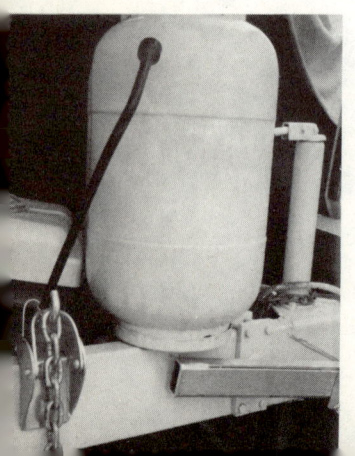

Plate 20. Raise chain to top position.

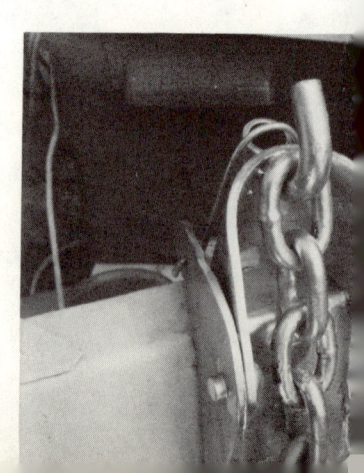

Plate 21. Secure the wire latch so chain can't fall.

Plate 15. Lower jack post until ball is in socket.

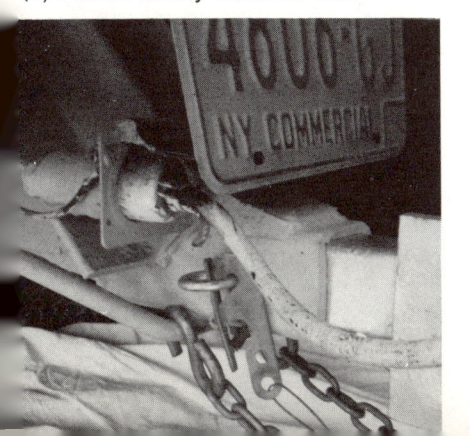

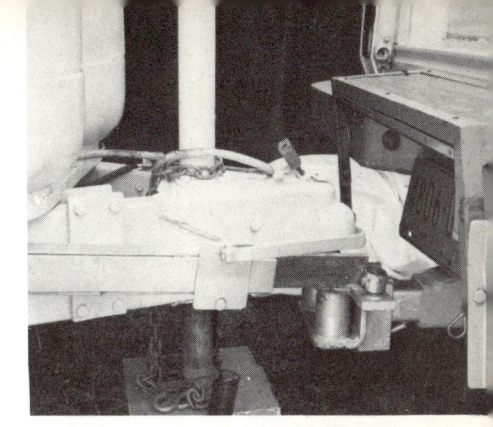

Plate 16. Flip locking lever down and secure it with padlock or bolt. Place sway bar on its ball and secure it with spring clip.

Plate 22. (1) Insert electric plug. (2) Attach break-away wire to car. (3) Attach safety chain to car.

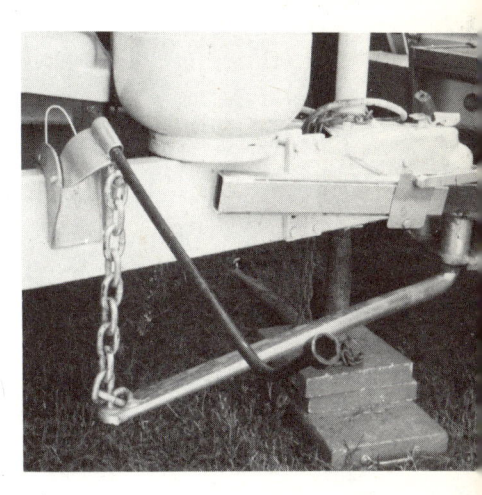

Plate 23. Hookup complete; tighten sway bar. Finally, raise jack post and store wooden blocks.

Testing Trailer Lights

When you connect the electric plug, you might find you still have no lights, turn signals, or brakes. The first thing to do is check the in-line fuses. If they are okay and *nothing* works, the chances are that it is the ground connection that is corroded. A small flat file or small knife blade will clean off the corrosion in the plug or socket. But the problem could also be the ground connection to the car or trailer chassis. Battery current is only 12 volts, and a little corrosion will insulate it. Try wiggling the plug in the socket.

The trouble is more often in the trailer plug than in the car socket. The trailer plug is exposed to the weather, while the lid on the car socket protects it from rain, dust, pollen, tree sap, salt air, and whatever else might corrode it. I tried putting a tight-fitting can over the plug, but it worked poorly. It kept the dust and dirt out, but it also kept the condensation in, which speeded corrosion. Then I tried wrapping the plug with a thin piece of foam rubber (the kind you get in variety stores) about ⅛-inch thick. (We also use it to line the back of the trailer shelves.) I tied the foam rubber over the plug with garden plant ties or rubber bands (but rubber bands do not last very long when exposed to sun and weather). Then I laid the plug back in between the propane tanks where the rain can't run down the cable into the plug. Since then we have never had a corroded plug. The foam rubber keeps out the dust and dirt, but since it is porous, it allows condensation to evaporate.

If you still don't get current to your trailer, but your car lights go on, you know the battery and connections are okay. The next thing is to find out if the trouble is in the car wiring or in the trailer wiring. Since the car lights and signals go on, you know the car fuses are not blown. Now is the time to use your 12-volt test light. You can buy a 12-volt test light at an auto supply store, or you can make one with a 12-volt bulb and socket with two wire leads (Figure 21).

Attach one lead to the car chassis as a ground (an alligator clip works well) and touch the other lead to each prong in

Hooking Up 65

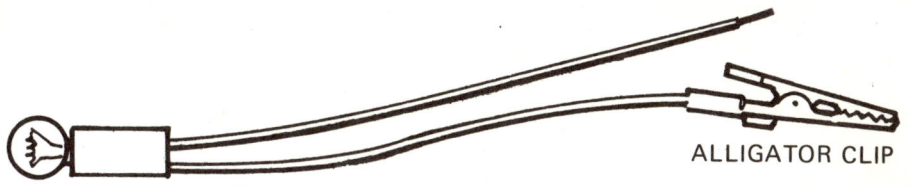

Fig. 21. Test light used to check wiring

the car socket while your partner first turns on lights, then turn signals, and then presses on the brake pedal. In this way you can find out which circuits are not working and trace any wire that does not have current. If the "hot" line isn't working, check the fuses at each end of the line.

If all the circuits are working, the trouble must be in the trailer wiring. Put the trailer plug into the car socket. At the end of the trailer cable there should be a connection box (Plate 24). Sometimes the connection box is inside the trailer.

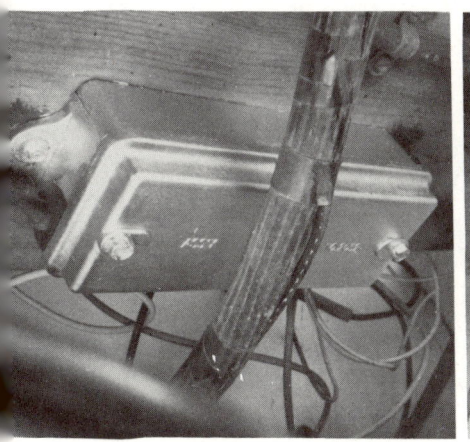

Plate 24. Left, on this trailer the connection box, at the end of the trailer cable, is located under the battery, behind the propane tanks. Plate 25. Right, same connection box with cover off. All wires from the plug connect to one row of terminals. All wires from trailer connect to the other row.

Take the cover off (Plate 25). Attach your test light to "ground" on the trailer frame, and touch each wire from the plug in the connection box with the other lead, while your partner turns on car lights, turn signals, and brakes. Then you will know if current is getting through the cable. If one or more of the circuits are dead, try taking the plug apart to see if there are loose or corroded connections in the plug. If any lights are not working, you might have a burned-out bulb or a corroded contact in the bulb socket. Whatever the problem, the steps just described will almost certainly find the trouble. The only other possibility—a broken wire inside the trailer wiring—is very remote. I have never known such a case, but if it should happen, the only thing to do would be to disconnect the terminals of the broken wire and run a new one.

If everything is working, you are nearly ready to go, but check everything once more. Walk around the trailer and look underneath. Sewer hose tube cover fastened? Cover on sewer pipe? Back trunk locked? Door step pushed in? All windows and vents closed? 110-volt electric cable stowed properly? All jacks, leveling boards, and wheel chocks stowed away? Jack post cranked all the way up?

The Propane Connection

If you have a gas refrigerator, water heater, and furnace, the question arises: "Should I turn off the propane while traveling?" One answer is that we have never known a trailerite who turned off his propane tanks. We have talked with hundreds of people, and all of them wanted to keep their refrigerator going. Many of them wanted to keep their water heater going as well. Sometimes the water heater pilot light blows out while we are traveling, because of gusts of air caused by passing trucks, but the refrigerator burner has never gone out. The refrigerator burner is well protected by a metal shield, so that it is not easily affected by the air blasts. The water heater has only a pilot light going most of the time, and it is small and easily blown out. Although it is usually protected by a metal shield, an air blast can blow right through the heater vent back to the pilot flame. There isn't much you can do about that except light it again. Some people put a furnace filter inside the cover, which may help.

Hooking Up

The furnace has never been a problem for us because we are usually in a warmer climate. But even in the South it sometimes freezes, so there have been a few times when we have left the heater on, too.

We have a shut-off valve to turn off the gas line to the cook stove (Plate 26). The shut-off valve turns off the pilot light for the top burners and the oven pilot, and that is really the main reason for turning off the gas. In case of a leak, the pilot could set off an explosion. The pilots for the water heater and furnace are vented to the outside and would not cause an explosion unless the furnace itself was faulty. The refrigerator burner is in a compartment separated and closed off from the inside of the trailer and probably could not ignite escaping gas unless the leak were in the gas line under the refrigerator.

Plate 26. Gas shut-off valve on stove is usually next to the top burners. On some models, stove top does not lift up; in that case valve can be placed at any convenient place in the copper tubing.

All gas appliances have safety devices that shut off the gas if the pilot flame (or the refrigerator burner flame) is extinguished. Because these devices are so reliable, we think that any danger from leaving the gas turned on is very remote. What little danger there might be could only occur as a result of an accident on the road that ruptured the gas line. With the gas tank valves open, the gas would pour out of the rupture and might be ignited by a spark, just as gasoline is sometimes ignited. Even in road accidents igniting of propane is rare, but it has happened. Propane tanks are not allowed in tunnels leading into Manhattan because a serious accident once occurred in a tunnel. There are other tunnels that limit the size of the propane tanks to 20 pounds. So there is some danger, however remote.

I am told that there are cases on record of gasoline vapor being ignited by refrigerator burners or hot water pilots while gasoline tanks were being filled, but we have never known anyone who had such an experience.

This is as good a time as any to tell you a little more about propane and butane. Commercially, propane is often referred to as LP gas, meaning liquefied petroleum gas, which is usually a mixture of propane and butane. Under pressure both propane and butane are liquids. As the temperature rises, the liquids turn into gases, but the propane boils (turns into a gas) at $-40°$, while butane boils at $+32°$. Below freezing, butane stays liquid, so no gas comes through the pipe to heat the trailer or cook dinner. But propane will continue to supply gas at temperatures down to 40° below zero. You will probably never know just what is in your "propane" tank, because oil companies supply whatever is needed for the particular locality where it is sold, just as they do with winter and summer gasoline.

We will just keep calling LP gas "propane." It is highly inflammable, potentially explosive, and very poisonous. However, accidents attributed to propane, involve an extremely small percentage of all the trailers on the road—a tribute to excellent safety devices. Nevertheless, you should be informed of the possible dangers.

Because propane is a heavy gas, heavier than air, it settles to the ground unless air currents mix it around. It is almost indispensable to the trailerite, but it is nothing to take chances with. People have been killed in their sleep by propane leaks, and gas leaks have caused more than one trailer to blow up. Normally, propane is colorless and odorless, but commercially sold propane has an odor added that smells like garlic or onions. Your nose can detect as little as 1 part in 1,000,000, so you get plenty of warning before the gas concentration can build up to explosive or lethal proportions. A gas leak inside a trailer can make a bomb out of it. The gas mixes with the air in the trailer, and it is the mixture that is explosive. After enough gas has escaped, a spark or pilot light sets it off, and the whole trailer explodes like a grenade.

You can check all your gas connections with some soapy water and a paint brush. Brush the soapy water all around the connection and watch for bubbles. Never check for a gas leak with a lighted match. That seems so obvious that I feel foolish even mentioning it, but some people keep doing it.

If you smell gas inside the trailer, open the door as well as the windows. Since the door opening is lower than the windows, the gas will flow out at the lower level.

Even without a gas leak, a gas flame can kill people. As I write this, we have a report of three people sleeping in a trailer in a campground. It was a cold winter night. In order to provide a little heat, they turned on the gas burners of the stove and then went to bed. The trailer was shut tight, the gas flame used up all the oxygen, and the three people were asphyxiated. Of course, that happens in homes and apartments, too. So, for the benefit of those who haven't heard it before, I'll repeat the warning: Do not go to sleep with an unvented gas flame on, and keep at least one window open. I am afraid, however, that people who have such accidents never read anything, because the warning has been published over and over again.

This warning does not apply to gas heaters that are properly installed in travel trailers. All of these heaters use outside air, and the burnt gases are vented outside.

Fires do happen in trailers, as well as in homes—so protect yourself with fire extinguishers. There are several kinds: (1) dry chemical, (2) carbon dioxide, (3) foam, and (4) carbon tetrachloride. From the standpoint of cost, efficiency, and size, the most practical for a travel trailer or other recreational vehicle is the dry chemical type (Plate 27). The 2¾-pound size costs in the neighborhood of $12 to $14. It is a cylinder about 14 inches high and is suitable for any kind of fire—propane, electrical, gasoline, grease fire in the kitchen, or simply a fire caused by smoking.

Plate 27. Dry chemical fire extinguisher installed in a corner over the refrigerator in trailer kitchen.

The CO_2 and foam types are also excellent, but they are much bulkier to carry and more expensive. The carbon tetrachloride type should never be used. It is too dangerous. When heated, the carbon tetrachloride breaks down into CO_2 and chlorine gas, both of which effectively smother a flame; but the chlorine gas can cause severe lung trouble or death, especially in an enclosed space like a trailer.

We carry three dry chemical extinguishers, two in the trailer (one near the kitchen and one in the bedroom) and one in the cab of the tow truck. In the cab, it is placed where we can get to it fast—on the wall next to the passenger's right foot (Plate 28).

You couldn't buy cheaper insurance.

Plate 28. Dry chemical fire extinguisher in the truck, where it can be reached quickly.

9

Before You Leave Home

When you are ready for a long trip, there are a number of things to be done before you leave. Two frequently asked questions are (1) "How do you cash checks, or what do you do about carrying money?", and (2) "How do you arrange for mail?"

Money
We experimented with several money methods. First, we tried traveler's checks and found them a big nuisance. Besides, you eventually use up your supply, and what do you do then? Incidentally, we found a few places that would not accept traveler's checks.

Then we established a joint bank account with one of our sons. When we found we were running short, we would write or telephone him to send us cashier's checks from the bank. Some banks would not cash them, although we did find some that would. In places where we were not known, cashing cashier's checks was difficult, and personal checks were out of the question.

Before You Leave Home

Finally, we asked our son to send us postal money orders. These can be bought in any denomination up to $100 at a cost not much different from that of traveler's checks. Postal money orders can be cashed at any post office in the United States by showing your driver's license for identification. On several occasions we have had to go back in the afternoon because small post offices did not have enough cash on hand in the morning. But we have never had a moment's trouble cashing them.

Social Security checks can be cashed in any bank, and most tellers are friendly and cordial. Driver's licenses are sufficient identification. Once or twice we found a stuffy bank that required us to get the approval of a bank officer, but that took only a moment.

Mail

Now, about mail. Since our son offered to forward our mail, we left a notice at the post office to send all mail to his address. We notified our friends, bank, insurance companies, and others of our new permanent mailing address, and we ordered return address stickers for our own envelopes printed with our son's address. Whenever we get to a place where we intend to stay for a while, we telephone or write our son to send the mail to our temporary address. Sometimes our address is c/o General Delivery.

Mail handling has been easy for us, but it might not be so easy for people who have no relatives or friends willing to forward mail. We have met a few trailerites who are in that predicament, and they tell us that they employ a mail-forwarding service. They also tell us that they have found it very reliable and not expensive. We have seen advertisements for such services in trailer magazines, but we have never had any need for them.

Pre-Departure Checklist

If, unlike us, you have a permanent home, you will want to make various other arrangements before leaving. Here is a checklist to help you remember:

- Stop delivery of newspapers, milk, or anything else that is regularly delivered. Any accumulation of papers on your porch is a tip-off to burglars.
- Fill out a post office card to hold or forward mail.
- Leave a key with a neighbor and give him a mailing address where you can be reached or the address of a relative who will know where you are at all times.
- Put telephone on vacation service, if it is available.
- Be sure all gas jets are turned off, or better yet, turn off gas at the meter.
- If you are going to be away from home during the winter (and you live in a cold area) you will need to either (1) turn the heat down very low, just so water pipes don't freeze (in this case, a neighbor should check it regularly); or (2) turn off the water and drain all pipes, traps, toilets, radiators, boiler, water storage tank, etc. Get a plumber for this job unless you are sure you know how to do it.
- Get rid of all old paper, rags (particularly oily ones), or other trash that could cause a fire by spontaneous combustion.
- Be sure your car and trailer insurance is paid up and all in order. If you are going to Canada, get a nonresident liability insurance card from your insurance company.
- Remove food from refrigerator. Turn it off and leave it open.
- Arrange for care of pets, house plants, garden, and lawn.
- Put any valuables you are not taking with you in a safety deposit box.
- Leave your shades up and get a 24-hour timer. Set it so that some lights go on at winter sundown time and off at bedtime.
- Leave closet doors open to prevent or minimize condensation.

We also have checklists of things to be done inside and outside the trailer before traveling. Such lists come in handy after we have been parked for a while, because when we get ready to move again, we are likely to forget some important details. When we first started trailering, we stopped for lunch one day and found the cupboard doors open, canned goods spilled out, and flour, sugar, and honey all over everything. I hope the following checklist will help you avoid such an unpleasant episode.

Inside the Trailer

- Close all windows and ceiling vents.
- Put a dowel through all drawer pulls on the vanity so that the drawers won't open (Plate 29).
- Tighten nylon cord around everything in the cupboards (Plate 29). We put nylon cord in all cupboards, attached to screw eyes in the back corners, as shown in Figure 22.
- Place pin in refrigerator door.
- Place TV, radio, clock, and other loose articles on bed. Cover with pillows and blankets.
- Put chairs on front couch. (We have folding chairs but have found it easier to put them unfolded on the seat across the front of the trailer.)
- Put padding around lazy Susans (We have them in the corners of the cupboards.)
- Turn off gas stove valve and put down stove cover. (If you don't have a stove cover, you can take the grates off and store them or put a blanket over the top of the stove with the pilot off.)
- Put table down.
- Secure sliding mirrors in bathroom cabinet. (We put a piece of stiff wire between the knobs to keep the mirrors from sliding.)
- Put toilet seat down.
- Switch refrigerator from electricity to gas.
- If you keep a log book, mark down the starting mileage.

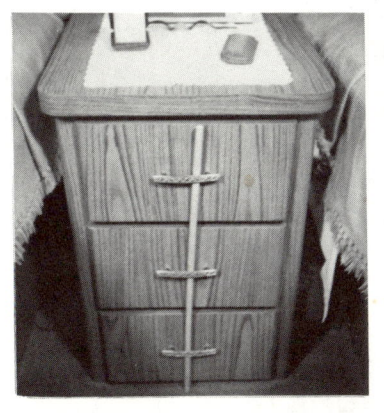

Plate 29. Left, dowel through drawer pulls keeps drawers from sliding out. Plate 30. Right, even if kitchen cabinet doors come open, the tightened cord keeps groceries where they belong.

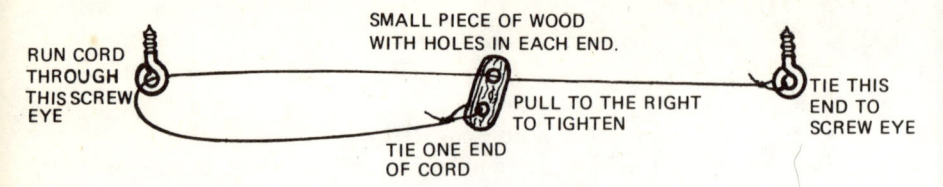

```
RUN CORD        SMALL PIECE OF WOOD
THROUGH         WITH HOLES IN EACH END.
THIS SCREW                                      TIE THIS
EYE                     PULL TO THE RIGHT       END TO
                             TO TIGHTEN         SCREW EYE
                        TIE ONE END
                         OF CORD
```

Fig. 22. Attaching retaining cord to kitchen cabinet

Outside the Trailer

- Warm up the car, put on and adjust mirrors.
- Take down the TV and radio aerials.
- Wash out drainage bucket or disconnect and stow sewer hose. Put cap on pipe.
- Take awning down and put front and rear rock-guard awnings down.
- Remove jacks from under the trailer, but do not remove wheel chocks until hookup is completed. If you are on a slope, the trailer could start moving.
- Disconnect and stow electric cable.
- Disconnect and stow water hose.
- Raise trailer tongue.
- Secure ball mount in back of tow car and back it into position under trailer socket. Grease ball.
- Lower trailer and put on spring bars. Grease if necessary. (Do not grease cams.)
- Lock hitch clamp and raise tongue.
- Attach spring bar chains, pull them up, and secure the hook.
- Attach and tighten sway bar.
- Attach break-away switch wire.
- Attach safety chain.
- Plug in electric connector plug to car socket.
- Raise jack post all the way up. Remove the jack-post wheel, if any, and stow it along with any wood or plate you have used under the jack post.
- Remove and stow wheel chocks.
- Put rubber mat and step inside trailer. We carry an extra wooden platform to step on next to the trailer step (Plate 31).
- Push trailer doorstep in and lock door.
- Lock the back trunk.
- Drive off the leveling boards and stow them.

Before You Leave Home 77

- Take one last look. Walk around the trailer and look under it. Check all hitch connections and inflation of all tires.
- Check trailer signal lights, running lights, brake lights, and brakes.

Plate 31. A platform like this is convenient any time, but it is especially helpful when you are parked on a slope that raises the trailer step higher above the ground. Some trailerites hinge the top and store tools inside.

After you have performed all of the chores on the checklist, your hands could probably use washing, but the water hose is stowed away and there is no convenient way to do it. For this situation, we keep a can of waterless hand cleaner and a rag handy in the car trunk or camper. Waterless hand cleaner (available at most auto stores and some supermarkets) cleans grease off better than soap and water, is cheap, and lasts a long time.

10

Driving and Backing

You won't find driving with a trailer behind you much different from driving without a trailer. Of course, you will have considerably less acceleration. When you step on the gas, it will take longer, depending on the power of your engine, to accelerate to cruising speed. You should start slowly so that you don't jerk the trailer.

Turning
When you turn a corner, you will have to turn a little wider, because the trailer wheels will not track exactly behind the car wheels. The trailer will track to the inside of the turn, and the longer the trailer, the more space you must allow for inside tracking. Since most trailers are wider and their wheels are wider apart than car wheels, you have to stay a little farther away from the edge of the road.

On Grades
On up-hill grades, when your speed is reduced to 30 or 35 miles per hour, you should shift down to second. Lugging

your engine can cause it to heat up and use more gas, not less. If the grade is steep enough to slow you down to 15 or 20 miles an hour in second, shift down again. How much shifting you have to do depends on the power of the car engine, the weight of the trailer, and the steepness of the grade.

If your tow car is not properly equipped or is underpowered, and your engine heats up on an up-grade, turn off the air conditioner and turn on the heater. You may roast yourself on a hot August afternoon, but it is better than stalling or ruining your engine. Turning off the air conditioner takes a considerable load off the engine, and turning on the heater adds another cooling radiator. As soon as you get to a place where you can get off the road, stop and keep your foot on the accelerator for a fast idle, but do not race the engine. When the heat indicator needle goes down, or the idiot light goes out, you can turn off the engine and let it cool for half an hour.

If you can't do anything about getting a more suitable tow car, try driving only during the cooler hours. If you do trade in for a better tow car, ask about getting a heat gauge instead of an idiot light. You will find it much more satisfactory to know you are heating up while it is happening than after it has already happened.

On downhill grades long enough for you to keep gathering momentum, shift down to second and let the engine help with the braking (but not on wet or slippery roads, where you might jackknife). On very steep grades, shift into low gear. If you are still gathering speed, step on the brake pedal intermittently. It is better to pump the brakes occasionally than to keep the brake pedal down, even lightly, all the time. Doing so will cause the brakes to heat and fade.

It is easier to lose control on a downhill grade than on an uphill grade, so watch the speed. Most states have a lower speed limit for cars with trailers, and with good reason. Keep your speed down on slippery roads, use the hand brake-controller, and slow both the car and trailer with the *trailer brakes only*.

If you are going too fast, especially on slippery roads,

downhill, or on curves, you could jackknife your car and trailer. When you put on the car brakes, the inertia of the trailer will keep it coming and push the car around (Figure 23). If you are going fast, jackknifing can push you into oncoming traffic or turn you over. The most dangerous time is at the beginning of a rain or drizzle, when there is enough water to make the oil on the road slick, but not enough to wash it away.

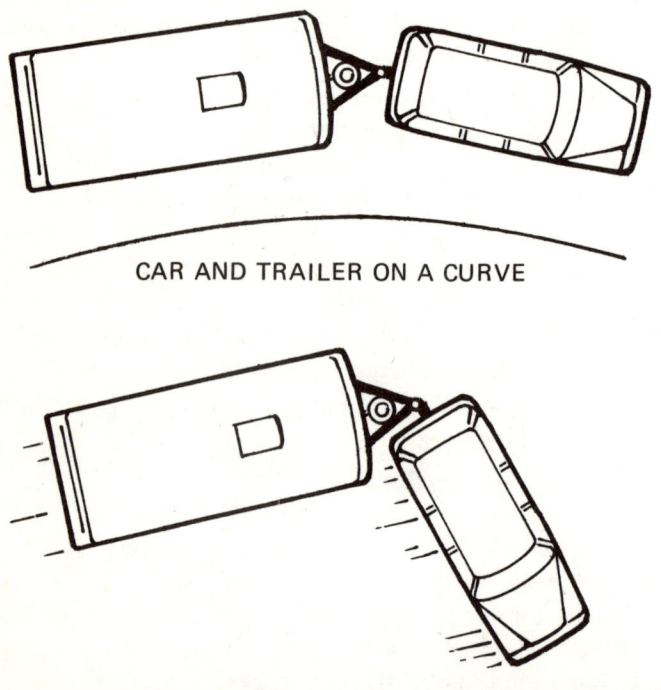

CAR AND TRAILER ON A CURVE

IF CAR BRAKES ARE APPLIED ON A SLIPPERY STREET, AND YOU ARE GOING FAST, TRAILER COULD PUSH THE CAR AROUND — WHICH IS CALLED JACKKNIFING.

Fig. 23. Jackknifing

If You Get Stuck

Sometime in your travels you will probably have to go

through sand or mud. When you do, keep going. If you stop, you will spin your drive wheel and dig in when you try to move again, especially if the sand or mud is soft. If you do get stuck, take your foot off the accelerator and keep it off, or you will just dig your wheels in deeper. The first thing to do is jack up the trailer tongue and take off the spring bars, or at least lengthen the chains so that they are no longer holding up the rear of the car. In this situation, you want all the weight you can get on your drive wheels.

Jack up the rear of the tow car, fill in under the rear wheels, and put wood or boards under and in front of the wheels. Dig in front of the trailer wheels, so that the path in front of the wheels is level for five or six feet and then slopes upward to the surface. Then, when you start again, keep going until you are out of the mud.

We always carry two five-foot boards. Fortunately, we have only had to use them once to get out of mud. We use the same boards as a work bench on two collapsible saw horses.

Another very handy thing to take along with you is expanded wire mesh—the kind used in buildings instead of plaster lath. We bought a standard-sized piece at a lumber yard, cut it into strips about 4 feet long and a foot wide, and packed the strips between pieces of corrugated board. We have used them a number of times—for ourselves and our neighbors—to get out of sand and off slippery grass or ice.

Side Mirrors

If you haven't used side mirrors before, you will get used to them in a very short while. On a passenger car you can get two kinds of mirrors: those that fasten just outside the doors or those that fasten up front on the fenders over the front wheels. Personally, I like the ones outside the doors because they provide a wider field of vision and they are low enough so that I can see over them. For me, the higher ones are confusing, especially at intersections, where I find myself looking at a rear view in the mirror instead of at the cross traffic.

Passing

When you pass another vehicle, it is going to take you longer to accelerate to passing speed, and your overall length will require more time to pass the other vehicle. That means that you have to be able to see very far ahead before you start to pass. Often that means that you will just have to wait behind a slow truck. On curving mountain roads you may have a long wait, so just relax and enjoy the scenery. Sometimes people will have to wait for you, too.

With a trailer behind you, it is more likely that cars will be passing you than that you will be passing others. If a line of cars starts to form behind you, pull off the road at the first opportunity and let them pass. In some states, there is a law stating that if there are as many as five cars behind a slow-moving vehicle, the slow vehicle must pull off and let them pass. It's the courteous thing to do in any case.

The overall length of your car and trailer can be anywhere from 30 to 50 feet. Allow this much space between you and the car in front for every 10 miles of speed. On expressways and interstates, keep over to the right and let the fast-moving traffic pass you. On such roads, 55 to 60 mph is about as fast as you should be going (55 mph maximum under the new fuel-saving regulation), and slower, of course, on two-lane roads.

When you see a stop light in the distance, you can save gasoline by slowing down so that the light will turn green again before you have to stop. You use the most gasoline starting from a dead stop.

Backing

The only real difficulty about pulling a trailer is backing. It's not really difficult—it just requires a bit of practice. When our first trailer arrived from the factory, the dealer hooked the trailer onto the back of the car and wished us good luck. We got in the car and started for home, a mile or two away. You might say I was nervous, but that wouldn't exactly describe my feeling—I was scared. But we got home without

Driving and Backing 83

incident and I felt elated. Then I spent the next half hour trying to back the trailer into the driveway. At first I would miss the driveway altogether, and when I finally got it off the street, the trailer wouldn't stay on the driveway ribbons, but instead insisted on going into the garden on one side, or onto the neighbor's lawn on the other. Eventually, persistence got it backed into a narrow space at the rear of the driveway. For our second lesson, we took the trailer to a supermarket parking lot on Sunday when it was clear of cars and practiced backing until I got the hang of it.

Strange as it may sound, the longer the trailer, the easier it will be to back. Short trailers start to jackknife more quickly, whereas longer trailers, with the greater distance between the trailer wheels and car wheels, turn more slowly.

To turn when you back up, you turn the steering wheel in

TRAILER MOVES TO LEFT

TRAILER MOVES TO RIGHT

Fig. 24. Backing a trailer

the direction opposite to the way you turn the wheel when backing the car alone. The easiest way to remember this is to turn the bottom of the steering wheel, nearest you, in the direction you want the rear of the trailer to go (Figure 24).

If you want to back into a trailer space, start with the tow car in the middle of the road, because as you turn you will be using *both* sides of the road (Figure 25). As the car backs toward the left side of the road, you will have to turn the steering wheel in the opposite direction, so that the car follows the trailer. If you don't get it just right the first time, pull up and back it again. It is easier if you can back it from the *left* side, so that you can look out your side of the car and see where the trailer is going. Whichever way you are backing, you can see only one side of the trailer, so you will usually need someone to direct you. Giving directions to the driver is also an art to be learned. The best way, we think, is for the person who is going to direct to motion by pointing left or right the direction the *back* of the trailer should go and to use the other hand to motion *forward* or *backward* or *stop*. Then he can tell you to "cut hard" or "follow" or "straighten up."

AS YOU TURN THE BOTTOM OF YOUR STEERING WHEEL TOWARD THE RIGHT, THE FRONT OF THE CAR FIRST MOVES TOWARD THE RIGHT.

THEN AS YOU CONTINUE BACKING, THE TOW CAR BACKS TOWARD THE LEFT SIDE OF THE ROAD.

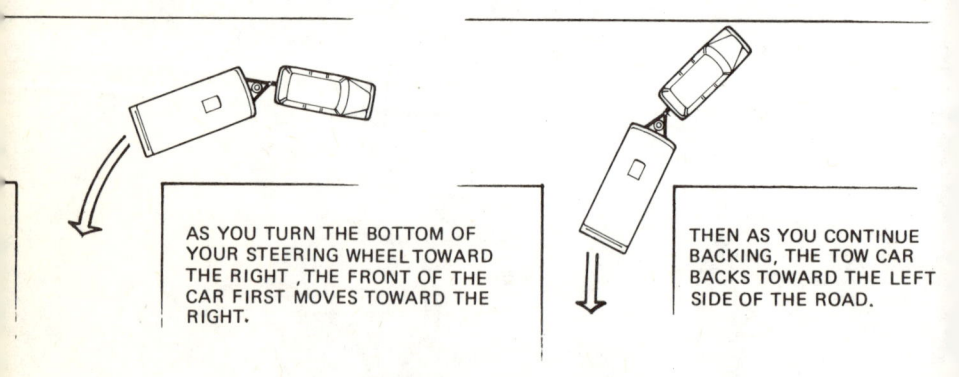

Fig. 25. Backing into a parking space

When you first try it, it's awkward. It just "ain't" natural. But a little practice is all that it takes. If you watch a truck driver, you will note that he backs up *slowly* and seldom has to do it twice. So take your time; you'll get parked a lot faster by going slowly.

When you first start learning to back into a turn, get out of your car a few times as you turn and inspect the rear of the tow car. Find out how sharp a turn you can make without mashing the bumper or fender into the trailer beam or propane tank. If you happen to be driving a pickup with a camper or camper cap, be sure the upper part of the camper doesn't hit the trailer (Figure 26). Some trailers are made with their fronts tilted forward, so that when you turn, the top rear corner of the camper will put a hole through the trailer. I saw a man working for a dealer put holes through

Driving and Backing 85

two trailers doing just that. If there is just a little clearance between the top of the camper and the trailer, you could still hit it if the ground were uneven (Figure 27).

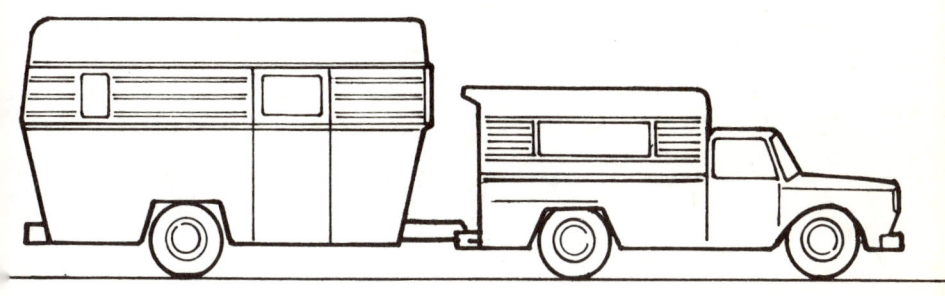

Fig. 26. Before you buy a cap for your pickup truck, be sure you have enough clearance between truck and trailer. If the front of the trailer is tilted forward, the corner of the truck might hit it when you turn.

Fig. 27. Even if the truck cap clears the trailer on a turn on level ground, it could still cause damage on an up-grade if clearance is too close.

11

When You Stop for the Night

Where to stop is the first question to be answered. There are now thousands and thousands of places for trailers, campers and motor homes to stay for a night or for months.

There are several widely circulated campground and trailer park guides that are available in trailer supply stores, book stores, and libraries. These guides also list national parks and forests, state parks, and private campgrounds. If you are not near a store or library, you can write for:

Good Sam Club: Recreational Vehicle Owner's Directory, published by The Good Sam Club, P.O. 500, Calabasas, California 91302

Rand McNally Travel Trailer Guide, published by Barcam Publishing Company, Box F, Palos Verdes Peninsula, California 90274

Or write for information from:

AAA
1712 G Street N.W.
Washington, D.C. 20006

An Overnight Stop

After you have pulled into your space at an overnight park or campground, what do you have to do? If your stay is to be just for the night, as little as possible. As soon as the car stops, Kay checks to see if the trailer is level sideways. If you have the usual absorption-type refrigerator, it will not work properly unless the trailer is level.

We carry quite a bit of wood, ⅜ inch and ¾ inch thick. From the position of the bubble in the level, my copilot can tell just how much wood will be needed under the wheels on one side. After looking at the level, she will tell me "two thick boards and one thin one on the left side." Then I get out four thick and two thin boards, put two thick and one thin either in front or in back of each of the two left wheels, and drive the trailer up on them. Then we check the level once again. Occasionally we may have to add or subtract a board to get it perfectly level. Sometimes (but not very often), we get into a space that is perfectly level, so that no wood is needed under the wheels.

Then we check the level front and back. Once in a while the trailer is perfectly level, or almost. If the front has to go up a little, we put a block of wood under the jack post and crank up the front of the trailer and the back of the car along with it. Of course, there is a limit as to how high you can jack it while it is hooked to the car. If it is too high or too low, you have to unhook. But that seldom happens.

If we are in a campground with no sewers we just put a bucket under the sewer pipe to catch the dishwater. When the bucket is full, we dispose of the dishwater down the campground toilet. Of course, the holding tank valve stays closed.

If we are in a trailer park where there are complete hook-ups, we connect the water hose, sewer hose, and electric cable, and we are all set for the night. Remember to lock the car.

We may or may not put up the front and back rock-guard awnings. These are fiber glass awnings that cover the front (and rear) windows of the trailer and can be raised when parked. They come as standard equipment on some models and are optional on others. Our decision depends largely on the view and the time of day (or night). We may put up the TV aerial if we feel like looking at TV. But we never unhook the car for one-night stops, unless the ground is so uneven that we are forced to do so, or unless we want to do some shopping.

If it gets too cool for comfort after the sun goes down, we often turn on the propane lights, which give off quite a bit of heat. On warm nights, when the heat from the propane lights would be uncomfortable, we use a fluorescent 12-volt light, which draws comparatively little current.

A Longer Stay

If we are going to stay for a few days or longer, of course we unhook the car. In order to unhook, you have to jack up the hitch as high as you can conveniently turn it, so as to release the tension on the spring bars. Be careful when you are letting the chains down. If the pipe or rod you use as a lever should slip out of your hand, it could slam down on your foot. This happened to an acquaintance when we were in Jasper, B.C. The piece of pipe whipped down on his foot and cut it seriously enough to delay his departure two days.

When the bars are off, let the tongue down and unlatch the locking lever. Jack up again, enough to clear the ball, disconnect all other connections, and pull the car a few feet away.

Don't forget the wire to the break-away switch. I forgot to unhook the break-away wire from the car once, and when I pulled the car forward a few feet, of course it pulled the pin out of the switch. However, I didn't know it until the next day. We weren't using the battery, because we were in a trailer park using 110 volts.

As soon as the pin was out, the brakes set and stayed set until the battery was completely discharged. I turned on the converter and charged the battery again, so no great harm was done, but had we been in a campground with no house current available, we would have had to take the battery to the nearest garage to get it charged up again.

After the trailer is unhooked, there are a few other things to be done. First we put a block of wood on the ground for the jack post to rest on. We like a nice, big, solid block, so that a gust of wind doesn't tip it over. Then we put stabilizing jacks under the trailer, two under the beams in the front, and two under the trailer beams in the rear. The only purpose of these jacks is to keep the trailer from bouncing on the springs. You can't, or shouldn't, try to level the trailer by jacking one side up higher than the other. If the ground is soft, we have wood to put on the ground, to set the jacks on. In fact, we have quite a number of square pieces of wood, so that we can build the platform under the jacks up to eight or ten inches high. If the ground slopes, the front or rear of the trailer can be quite high off the ground.

Here is a good way to put the stabilizing jacks under the trailer. First, lower the front of the trailer by turning the jack post screw about 10 turns. Then put the jacks under the rear so that the tops of the jacks just touch the beams, but don't tighten them. Next, raise the front of the trailer to level. Then place the front jacks and tighten them snugly. We put our front jacks about midway between the trailer wheels and the jack post.

Leveling the Trailer

When you park in an overnight trailer park, the spaces are usually fairly level. But in campgrounds, especially in mountainous areas—you will seldom find a level spot. We have been in spots in the Sierras where the trailer tongue was on the ground when we got through leveling. In other places, the tongue was way up in the air, and the rear of the trailer was close to the ground.

Extremely uneven ground can cause special jacking and leveling problems. When one end of the trailer is very low, the customary stabilizing jack won't fit under the trailer, so we carry two scissor jacks, which flatten out to only a few inches high. For the high end, as previously mentioned, we carry more square pieces of wood than we usually need, to make a high platform for the jacks.

Sometimes the wheels on one side of the trailer have to be raised as much as six or eight inches to make it level. For this purpose we carry wood cut in a special way. We use outdoor plywood, because it is strong in both directions and not likely to crack. We paint all the boards to preserve them, since they are outdoors and next to the ground. We cut them all eight inches wide and from 13½ inches to 21 inches long, so that when they are stacked, they form a ramp (Figure 28). The boards are alternately ¾ inch and ⅜ inch thick. With the wood stacked to form a ramp, we drill four holes in each stack to hold spikes. The holes are large enough so that the spikes slip through them easily. If you have a single-axle trailer, you can stack as many boards as you need to make the trailer level, and simply pull the trailer wheel up on the ramp. The spikes keep the stack from shifting when you drive up onto it.

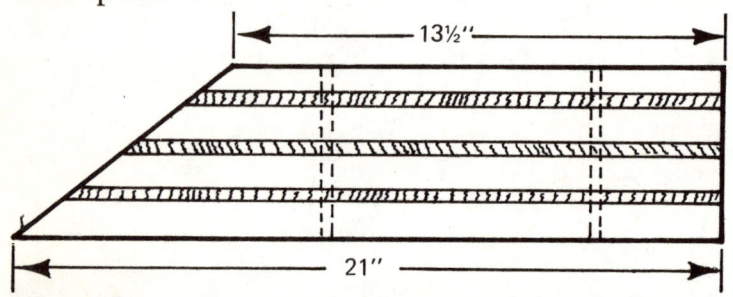

Fig. 28. Plywood boards can be stacked to form a ramp. They can also be used separately for leveling. Since the distance between tandem wheels is not standard, you may need boards shorter than 13½ inches.

Another method is to carry a tapered piece of wood and pull the trailer up on it to a point where it is level, then put a chock next to the wheels to keep the trailer from rolling back. This system works fine, but we prefer the first method, because the wood can be used under the jack posts or under the stabilizing jacks when needed.

We have a tandem-axle trailer, and two axles require that things be done a little differently. We have used the ramp

When You Stop for the Night 91

described above to change a flat tire, by pulling the good tire up on the ramp. This technique lets the flat tire drop down far enough so that it is easy to get it out of the wheel well.

But for leveling the side of the trailer when one side is very low, we use the boards as shown in Figure 29. When you cut the boards, be sure you have enough short ones—short enough to fit between the wheels.

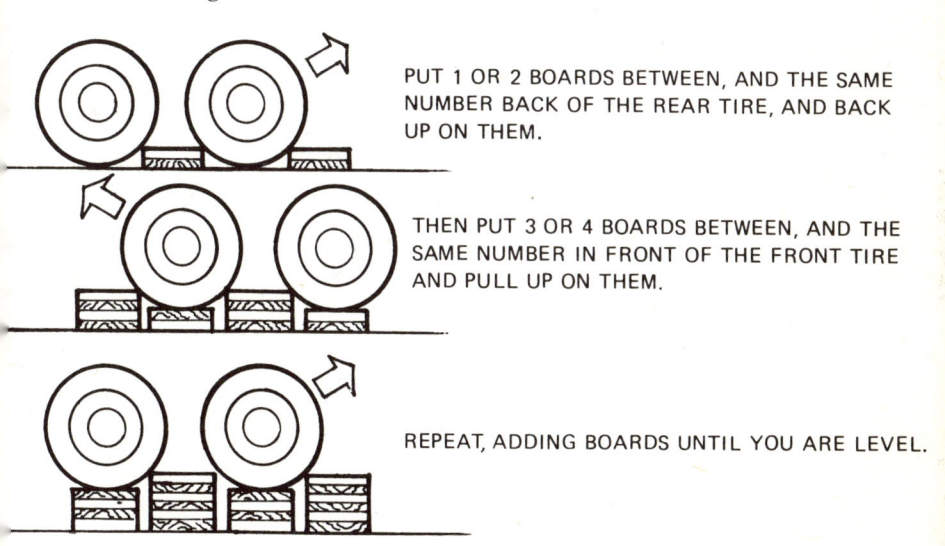

PUT 1 OR 2 BOARDS BETWEEN, AND THE SAME NUMBER BACK OF THE REAR TIRE, AND BACK UP ON THEM.

THEN PUT 3 OR 4 BOARDS BETWEEN, AND THE SAME NUMBER IN FRONT OF THE FRONT TIRE AND PULL UP ON THEM.

REPEAT, ADDING BOARDS UNTIL YOU ARE LEVEL.

Fig. 29. Leveling a trailer

If you are on a slope, you have to use wheel chocks to be safe. As soon as you unhook your car, you have no brakes. So, when you are leveling sideways, before the car is unhooked put chocks next to all the trailer wheels. We made some five inches deep out of plywood, glued and screwed together (Figure 30).

PUT THE CHOCKS UNDER ALL WHEELS. PUT THEM ON TOP OF THE LEVELING WOOD ON THE SIDE THAT IS RAISED.

CURVED TO FIT ARC OF WHEEL   Fig. 30. Wheel chock

Another, better kind of wheel chock is shown in Figure 31. Sometimes the tongue has to be raised higher than the

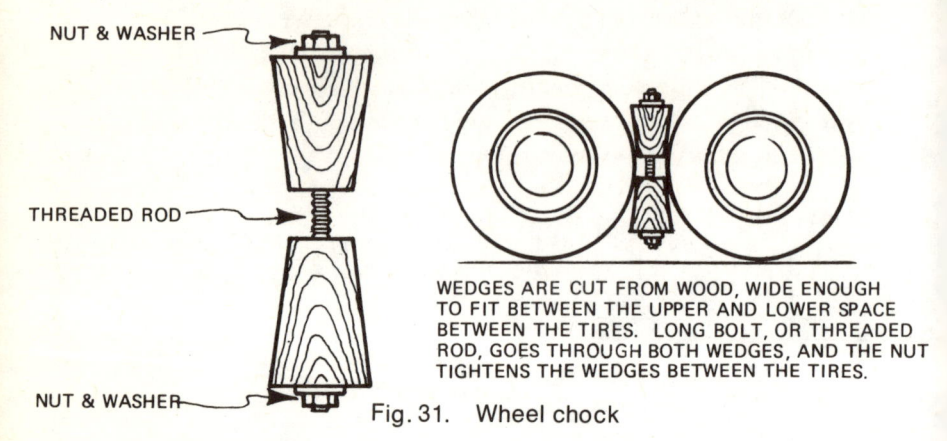

WEDGES ARE CUT FROM WOOD, WIDE ENOUGH TO FIT BETWEEN THE UPPER AND LOWER SPACE BETWEEN THE TIRES. LONG BOLT, OR THREADED ROD, GOES THROUGH BOTH WEDGES, AND THE NUT TIGHTENS THE WEDGES BETWEEN THE TIRES.

Fig. 31.   Wheel chock

jack post will raise it. In this case, raise the tongue with the jack post nearly as high as it will go and put another jack right at the socket, just to hold up the trailer. A car jack will do, or a stabilizing jack on a wood platform. Then raise the jack post and put more wood under it. Now crank the jack post until the trailer is level (Figure 32).

RAISE THE JACK POST AND PUT MORE WOOD UNDER IT.

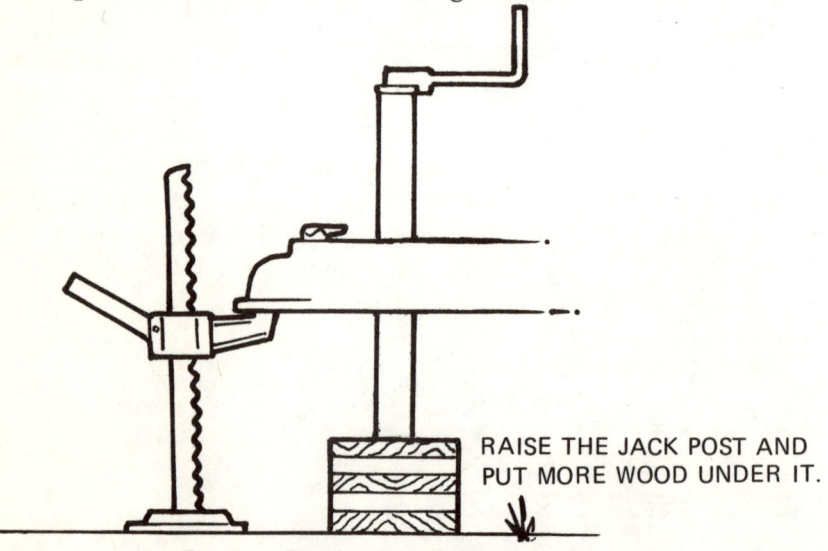

Fig. 32.   Raising the tongue to level a trailer

Tire Awnings

If we are going to stay more than a few days, we put on the trailer tire awnings. Trailer tires last much longer than car tires, simply because they are not used as much. It is quite likely that trailer tires will check and rot out before they wear out. Direct sunlight and heat are hard on rubber and will cause it to deteriorate much faster than if it is kept in the shade. In order to save our tires, we cover them with canvas tire awnings, which are simply canvas rectangles with rope sewn into a hem on top and bottom (Figure 33).

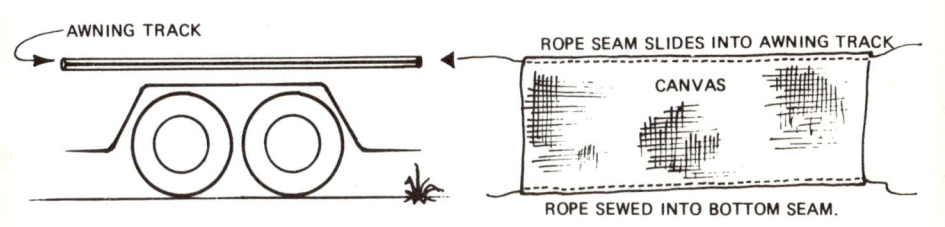

Fig. 33. Tire awning

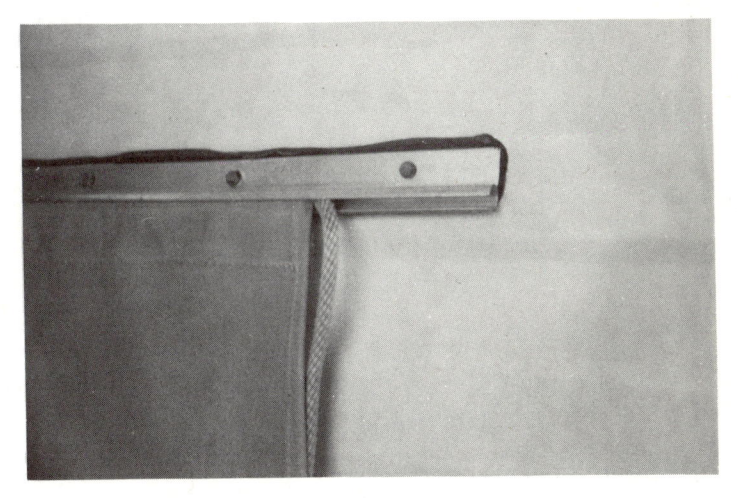

Plate 32. Awning track.

You can get awning track at a trailer store (Plate 32). To make tire awnings, cut two lengths of awning track long enough to cover both wheels, plus two feet longer. If the canvas were only as wide as the tires, the sun would slant in on them. The track is screwed on with the same kind of sheet metal screws used to put the aluminum panels on the side of the trailer, usually hex head no. 8, ¾ inch or 1 inch long. A ¼-inch hex socket driver makes the job easier. Put putty tape under the rail to keep water out of the screw holes.

Obviously, the finished awning should be deep enough to reach the ground. The canvas-covered rope slips into the awning rail, just as the trailer awning does. The bottom rope should be longer, so that it sticks out about two feet at either end, and the rope ends can be tied to stakes in the ground to secure the awning when the wind blows (Plate 33).

Plate 33.   Tire awning in place.

Gas or Electricity?

When you are stopping overnight, or for a few days, should you switch your refrigerator from gas to electricity? No. Keep it on gas unless you are going to stay for at least two weeks. When the gas is off, specks of dust and soot from the chimney can drop into the orifice. When you light it again, you might find that the box doesn't work as well as it did. Because the propane orifice is so small—about the size of a whisker—a very tiny speck of dirt or grease will affect it.

The electrical heating coil does cause the refrigerator to operate consistently better than the gas flame, so when we are going to stay for an extended period, we switch to electricity. But in that case, put a piece of metal foil over the burner so that it is completely covered. At the bottom of the burner tube there are air holes that need to be covered as well as the top. To cover the burner, you have to open the outside door and remove the metal shield that protects the flame from blowouts.

Because electric rates and the cost of propane vary widely in different parts of the country, we can't tell you which is cheaper; it depends on where you are. But if you are going to stay quite a while, we suggest that you switch to electricity even if it is more expensive. The difference isn't that great, and besides, it is cheaper than having food go bad.

When the refrigerator is operated on gas, you do have to clean the orifice occasionally—maybe once in six months. When it is on electricity, you can forget about it. After some years of use, the electric heater coil will burn out, but it is not a hard job to replace it. We will tell you more about keeping your refrigerator in good operating order in a later chapter.

Trailer Awnings

If you are going to stay put for a while, no doubt you will want to put up an awning. Incidentally, if you have a choice, place your trailer so that the hot afternoon sun will not be on the refrigerator side of the trailer.

There are several different types of awnings available. One type rolls up on the side of the trailer. Some have a support bar that extends out from the side of the trailer and gets in your way when you walk toward the front or rear. We have seen some of this type with red ribbons tied on the bar as a warning not to bump your head. Others have upright support posts that must be held with ropes and stakes.

If you are feeling rich, there is a roll-up type that is all electric. Just press a button and the awning rolls out (but the support bars are still in your way). All you have to do manually is tighten a couple of screws on the support bars after the awning is extended. It retracts just as easily. I don't know enough about the electrically operated awnings to recommend them to you, but they appear to be well designed and well built. For overnight stops, they would seem to be ideal. If a wind came up, you could simply push the button. Or, if you were going shopping, you could retract the awning while you were away and not have to worry about a wind coming up in your absence.

Another type is a canvas awning that slips into an awning track, with the outer edge held up by upright posts and with ropes tied to stakes in the ground to hold up the posts.

A third type is a metal frame awning that also attaches to the trailer by slipping into an awning track. A metal rod, put together in sections, goes through a seam in the outer edge. Upright adjustable posts hold up the metal rod. Additionally, metal rods with springs in them fit between the outer edge and the awning rail on the trailer.

Plate 34. Left, putting up an awning is a job for two people. One feeds the awning into the awning track, while the other, right, pulls it into position (Plate 35).

When You Stop for the Night 97

If you are going to be traveling frequently, the roll-down type *can* be easier to put up, but *not necessarily*. If you have to climb up and unroll the awning by hand and assemble the rods, it can be harder than sliding the edge of the awning into the awning track, and getting it rolled up again is worse. If the rolling and unrolling is done by a crank or spring-loaded device, it can be quite easy. But be sure you get a demonstration before you buy one. Awnings that are held up by ropes are considerably cheaper than framed awnings and it takes about the same time to put them up.

The big advantage of the metal-frame awning is that it is very stable in a wind—far more than any of the other kinds. There are a few more metal rods to carry, but you can buy a canvas sack, or tube, to put them in. The total space they occupy is very small.

Since we stay in one place for long periods at a time, we prefer a metal-frame awning, because once it is up we want to leave it up until we leave. Ours has been up in what the

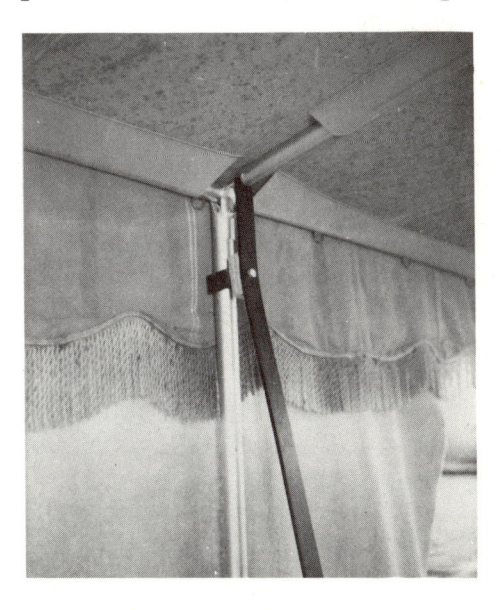

Plate 36. This awning tool makes it easy to put up a frame awning.

Weather Bureau said were 60 mile-per-hour winds, and it never budged. There is one difficulty, however, and that is pulling back the spring-loaded rods so that they fit into the slots of the uprights. The springs were so strong that we could not manage them without another person's help. We solved this with a simple lever.

One end of the top support rods (rafters) is flattened and simply pushes into the trailer awning rail under the awning. The other end fits into a slot in the upright pole (Plate 36). This end has a strong spring that pushes the awning out and keeps it taut, and the spring must be pulled back in order to slip the rod into the slot. This spring is purposely made strong to keep the awning steady and firm in a strong wind. The spring tension can be increased by turning either the screw or the rod. The end of the rafter pole is shown in Figure 34.

FLAT END FITS INTO NOTCH IN UPRIGHT POLE. SCREW CAN BE SCREWED IN OR OUT TO ADJUST TENSION.

AWNING TOOL IS ATTACHED AT END TO FIT AROUND SCREW.

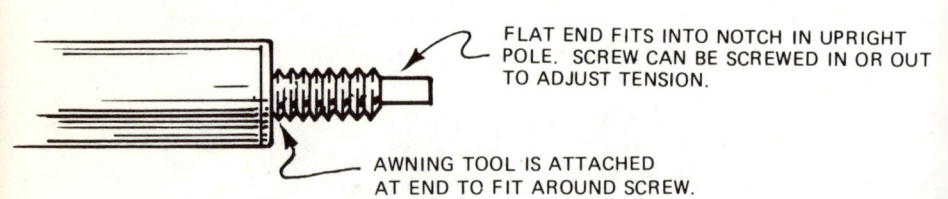

Fig. 34. End of awning support rod

We made a tool to pull back the spring-loaded rod from a piece of 3/16-inch steel, 1¼ inches wide and 32 inches long. Quarter-inch steel would be better, or a piece of angle iron, but the measurements aren't critical (Figure 35).

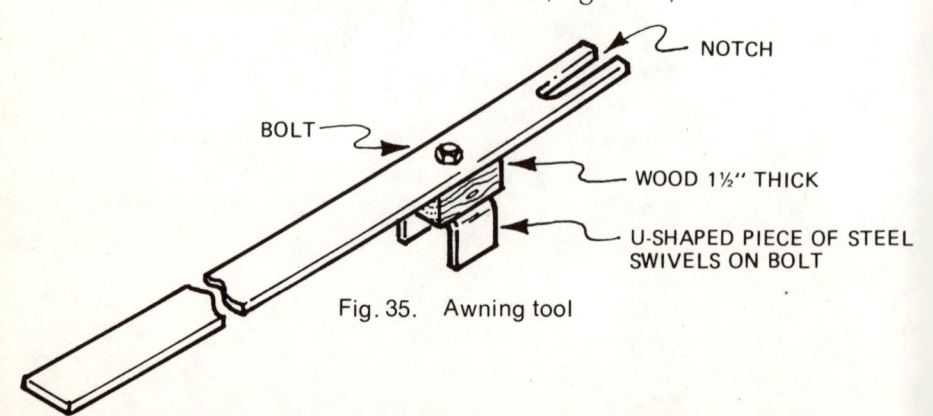

NOTCH

BOLT

WOOD 1½" THICK

U-SHAPED PIECE OF STEEL SWIVELS ON BOLT

Fig. 35. Awning tool

The "U" on the tool is placed over the upright pole and swiveled to one side, so that the notch in the tool will fit around the screw on the end of the rod. The spring is compressed by pushing down on the handle, which is then swiveled into position to drop the flat end of the screw into the slot.

Water Bottles

If you are going to stay in a campground where you have to carry your water, it is a good idea to save the plastic one-gallon bottles that bleach (or distilled water) comes in. Make a funnel by cutting one of the bottles in half and turning it upside down. With the funnel you can fill the bottles from the pump or faucet more easily. Keep one of the filled bottles in the trailer for cooking and washing, so you don't have to fill the water tank so often. Incidentally, that will save the battery, since the compressor or pump will go on less often. Keep another half-dozen bottles just outside the trailer door for handy replacement. We also have two three-gallon jugs, but these are heavier to carry and more awkward to handle.

Dry Firewood

We have often found it helpful to carry a dozen sticks of dry firewood with us. If you arrive at a campground that is soaking wet, it is much easier to get a fire started if you have some dry kindling. Don't forget to pack an ax or hatchet—a small saw comes in handy, too.

Tarpaulin Ground Cover

In campgrounds, you can avoid tracking dirt into your trailer by spreading a tarpaulin on the ground. We used an old painter's drop cloth and put grommets around the edge. Spikes driven through the grommet holes keep it down when the wind blows. Some friends who didn't have grommets drove the spikes through can tops.

12

Trailer Maintenance

Gas Appliances

Refrigerator. The gas or electric refrigerator in your trailer is not like the compressor type you have in your home or apartment. In the one you have at home, an electric motor furnishes the power to keep the cooling fluid (Freon) moving through its various parts.

Trailers use an absorption-type refrigerator. The heat energy is either a gas flame or an electric heating coil. The refrigerant is not Freon, but a combination of three fluids: water, hydrogen, and ammonia. All three are in a sealed system under great pressure—more than 200 psi. So, if it's not working properly, you can't cure it by adding refrigerant, as you might do with your automobile air conditioner.

To oversimplify the operation, the heat percolates the refrigerant fluids to the top of the system. The cooling fins cool the hot gases, which condense, and liquid ammonia solution flows into the evaporators in the freezer and refrigerator compartments, where it evaporates (which is what causes the cooling). The ammonia is again absorbed into the water solution and flows *by gravity* back down to the heater. There is a lot more to it technically, but that is the general idea, which is sufficient for trailering purposes. All you really want to know is how to keep the system working properly and how to fix it if it isn't.

The first thing to know is that the system needs the right amount of heat. If there is too much or too little, it stops working. There is not likely to be too much heat, because the pressure regulator on your propane tanks is adjusted to 11 column inches of water, and the maximum size of the flame is predetermined at the factory by the size of the orifice in the jet. It is a very tiny hole. Of course, the pressure regulator could get out of adjustment, and you could get too much gas pressure. That would cause a bigger flame and more heat. Less pressure would produce less heat.

An instrument called a *manometer* is used to check the gas pressure. You can borrow one from your gas company supply man, or you can quickly make one that is simple and accurate (Plate 37). Buy a few feet of clear plastic tubing at a

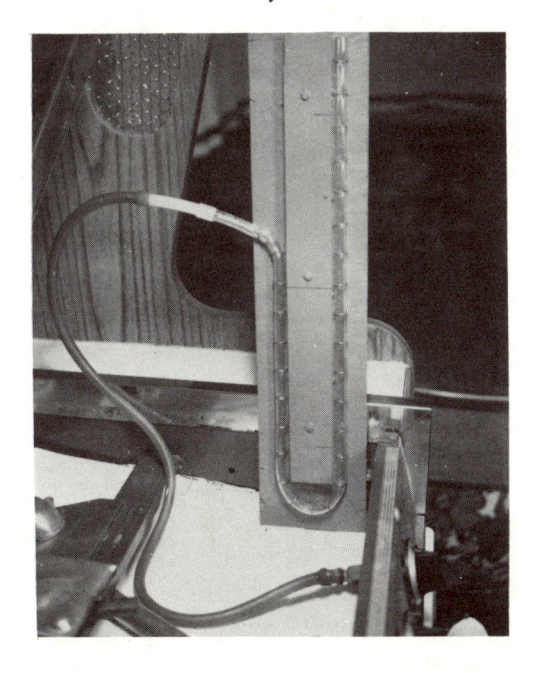

Plate 37. A homemade manometer is just as accurate as an expensive one.

hardware store; the tubing should be about ⅜ inch in outside diameter. Attach the tubing to a wood backboard. Small brads alongside the tubing will hold it in place, or you can drill holes in the wood and tie the tubing on with fishing line or thin wire. Attach a piece of soft, flexible rubber tubing to the end of the plastic tubing (just slip it over the end). The reason for using flexible rubber is that you can slip it over the gas connection. If you have trouble slipping the rubber hose on the tubing or gas outlet, lubricate it with a little wet soap.

Usually, the most convenient place to check the gas pressure is at the top burners of your stove. Take one of the burners out—you usually have to remove one or two screws, and the burner lifts right out. Put water in the plastic tube to the level indicated, attach the rubber hose to the gas outlet, turn on the gas very slowly, and measure the height of the water column (Figure 36). If you turn on the gas too fast, it will force the water out of the top of the tube.

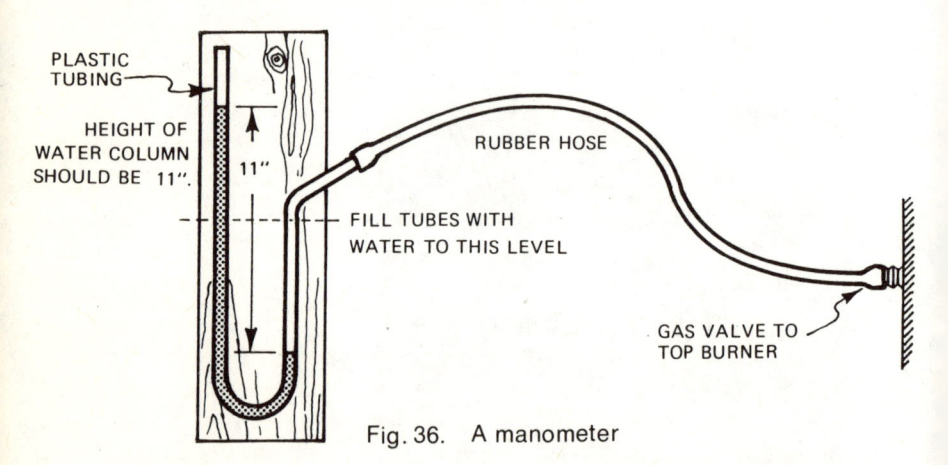

Fig. 36. A manometer

If your gas pressure is either too high or too low, you can easily adjust the pressure regulator, which is the disc-shaped device to which the copper tubing from your propane tank is connected (Plate 38). On the back of the disc is a screw cap. Unscrew the cap and, with a knife blade or wide-blade screwdriver inserted into the adjusting slot, turn it in or out until you get the right pressure. (You might have to use a mirror

Trailer Maintenance 103

to see the slot.) Turn it slowly, and have a helper look at the manometer and tell you when you are right on 11 inches. Once you know your pressure is okay, you won't have to think about it again for a long time.

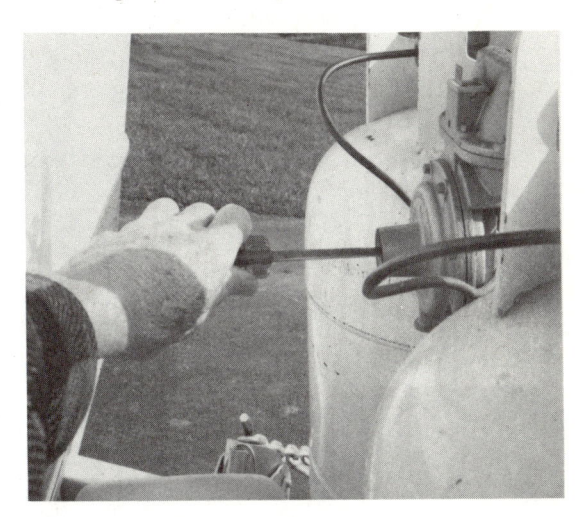

Plate 38. The gas pressure regulator almost always faces toward the back of the propane tank assembly—between the tanks and the trailer. Photo shows how to adjust the pressure.

Always be sure to level your trailer when you stop. If it is not level, the refrigerant may get trapped in the upper parts of the system and stop circulation. That problem will usually clear up when you level the trailer. But once in a while it won't. If a vapor lock develops and circulation stays stopped, in a 24-hour period the inside of your refrigerator may be as warm as the outside. There are two things you can do if that happens. Take the trailer out for a ride with the flame off. The movement will swish the refrigerant around and probably unlock the vapor lock. If that doesn't work, remove the refrigerator from its compartment and turn it on its side for 10 or 15 minutes; then turn it upside down and let it sit for a while. That will almost always unlock the vapor lock.

A word about getting the refrigerator out of its compartment: it is usually fastened with long screws at one side and at the bottom. The side screws go into the side wall of the refrigerator from the cabinet, or panel, or whatever is next to it. Sometimes it is difficult to locate the screws on the side, but the ones on the bottom are easy to find, as a rule. When all the screws are out, you can push the refrigerator out of its cabinet into the trailer from the opening on the outside. Of course, you have to turn off the gas and disconnect the gas line and the electric plug.

You may never have to do this if you keep your trailer level. If the trailer is going to be much out of level for quite a while, turn off the burner or electricity.

Incidentally, movement on the road doesn't affect the operation. As long as you are moving, the refrigerator keeps on freezing. Some older models occasionally have flames blown out by wind gusts. If yours blows out, you can rig up a shield of sheet metal to protect the flame. Or put a furnace filter inside the door while you are traveling.

The most likely cause of refrigerator trouble is a clogged jet, which cuts down the size of the flame and reduces the cooling. You will probably need to clean the jet every six months or so, in any case. Cleaning the jet is not difficult. The first thing to do is turn off the gas valve, which is usually next to the thermostat. Switch it over to electric operation if you have current available. Since different models are designed differently, it would not be practical to give you a detailed description of each one—even if I could—but they all work on the same principle. The burner is surrounded by a sheet metal shield to prevent the flame from blowing out. A couple of screws should take off the shield. The burner is directly under the chimney tube, and the jet is at the bottom of the burner, just below the air intake holes (Figure 37).

You may have to disconnect the gas line to the burner and the thin thermocouple line to get to the jet. The jet is simply a brass fitting with a tiny hole in the center through which the propane passes. Soak the jet in alcohol and then blow through the hole with compressed air or with a bicycle pump. If you don't have any way of blowing it out, you can use a very thin wire, but you must be careful not to enlarge

Fig. 37. Refrigerator gas burner

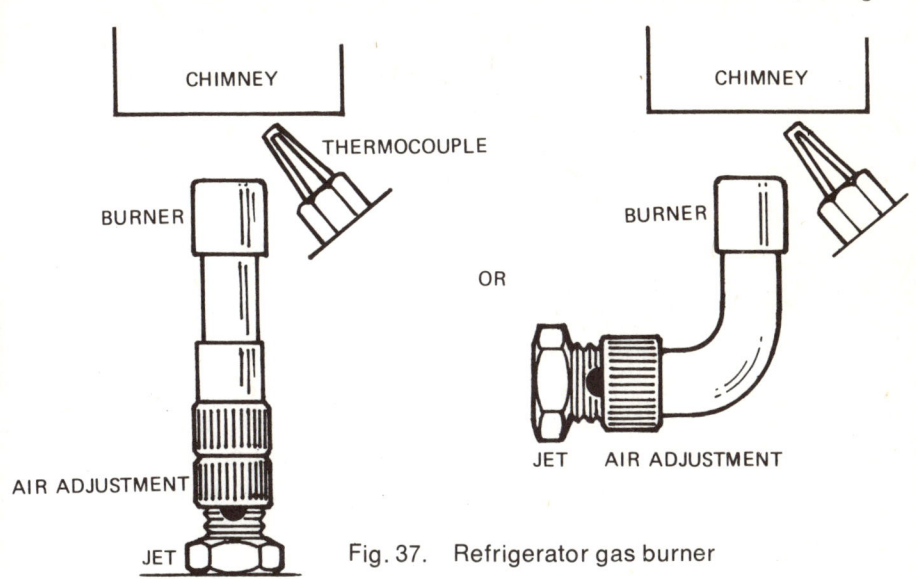

the hole. It wouldn't take much of an enlargement to make the flame too hot. While you're at it, clean the burner tube also, and then reassemble. Be sure the flame will be directly under the middle of the chimney; if it isn't, the cooling will be affected. The thermocouple should be in the flame, about ⅛ inch off center and about 3/16 inch to 5/16 inch above the top of the burner tube. Check the service manual that comes with the refrigerator for the exact position in your model. If you do not have a manual, write to the manufacturer for one.

The thermocouple generates a small electric current, enough to energize a magnet in the gas valve, which holds the valve open. If the flame goes out, the current stops and the valve closes, shutting off the gas. A very important and very reliable safety device.

The thermostat is attached to sensor tubes that run up into the refrigerator. The sensor tubes tell the thermostat when the box is too warm: the thermostat opens an internal gas valve, and the gas goes on full. When the sensors signal the thermostat that it is cold enough (depending on where you set the thermostat dial), the internal valve closes, and the flame cuts down to a very low level. There is a bypass route for the gas inside the thermostat that allows a little gas to pass all the time, but not enough to cause freezing. The valve inside the thermostat is entirely separate from the safety valve connected with the thermocouple. The flame stays small until the sensor tubes again call for more cooling, at which time the valve opens and the flame again goes to maximum. The flame is always at maximum or minimum—there is no in-between.

Another thing you must do to keep the refrigerator cooling properly is to keep the cooling coils and pipes on the back clean and free from dust. You should also keep the entire air passageway from the door louvers to the opening in the roof clear of obstructions. Sometimes there is a screen at the top under the roof cap that can get clogged. Birds have been known to build their nests there. Inside the louvered door some models have a screen that gets clogged. Anything that restricts the free-air flow over the back of the refrigerator will hamper the cooling.

When you are operating on gas, the flame adjustment is very important. Some burners are fixed at the factory and can't be adjusted. The air intake, on those that can be adjusted, should be adjusted so that the flame is all blue with a sort of crown of bright blue at the bottom of the flame. There should also be just a slight roaring sound, but not so much air that the flame becomes unsteady. An unsteady flame will result in poor cooling; so reduce the air until you get a steady flame, with a slight roar and a lighter blue crown at the bottom. Be sure you do not have a yellow-tipped flame (you have to use a mirror to see up into the chimney tube) because the yellow-tipped flame will deposit soot on the walls of the chimney. If that happens, the soot will act as an insulator, and not enough heat will get inside the generator.

If the inside of the chimney gets covered with soot, there is nothing to do but clean it out, and that can be a nuisance. It would be a five-minute job if you could get to it, because all you have to do is pull up the baffle wire at the top of the chimney and push a long brush down the chimney to clean it out. The whole difficulty is in getting to it. Some trailers have a door on the outside of the trailer, above the refrigerator. These are rare, but if you have one, all you have to do is open the door, pull up the wire in the chimney to which the baffle is attached, and push the brush down through the chimney. When we did it, we had a vacuum cleaner hose at the bottom of the chimney to suck up the black dust and soot. Then clean off the baffle, which is a piece of thin metal as wide as the diameter of the chimney, twisted into a spiral about six inches long. Its purpose is to fling the spiraling heat against the walls of the generator. When you put it back, be sure it is down all the way and the wire secured as before, so it can't drop any lower. It has to be in exactly the right place, exactly where the "boiler," or generator, is located.

If there is no way to get at the top of the refrigerator, which is usually the case, the next easiest thing to do is take the cap off the roof vent and work through the vent, which is plenty large enough for your arm to get through. Taking it off will probably break up the putty seal, so have some putty tape handy to replace it. You can get rolls of putty tape at any trailer or mobile home supply store. On some trailers this method would not work, because the roof vent is offset and you can't reach the refrigerator chimney tube from the roof vent.

The third way is to disconnect the refrigerator and take it out of the compartment.

Finally, to insure good cooling, be sure the door of the refrigerator closes so that the rubber gasket seals it completely all around.

In very hot weather, your refrigerator is not going to work as efficiently, no matter what you do, because the efficiency depends on the difference in temperature between the hot rear cooling coils and the air passing over them. But you can do several things to help. Take off the outside door, or open it up to allow more air to enter. You can even place a little electric fan at the bottom so that it blows up on the pipes—anything to speed up the air flow. Of course, you can't do that if you are out in a campground using a battery for electricity. Even if the fan only draws two amperes, the battery would be dead in a couple of days, unless you have a generator. Another thing that helps is to be sure the refrigerator side of the trailer is in the shade during the afternoon, when it is the hottest. If you can place your trailer so that the refrigerator side faces north, that would be ideal. And in very warm weather, try to get out everything you need and put everything away with as few openings of the door as possible.

If you have an air conditioner and you are connected to house current, you can keep your refrigerator operating in the hottest weather, just as if the temperature were 20 degrees cooler. Here's what you do: Take off the outside door and cover the louvers (Plate 39). You can use a sheet of brown paper cut from a shopping bag and tape it down with masking tape. You can't see the paper at all when you put the door back on. The paper will keep warm air from the outside from getting in. Then remove the little door under the refrigerator, the one you open when you want to light the burner or adjust the thermostat. Leave it off and store it somewhere.

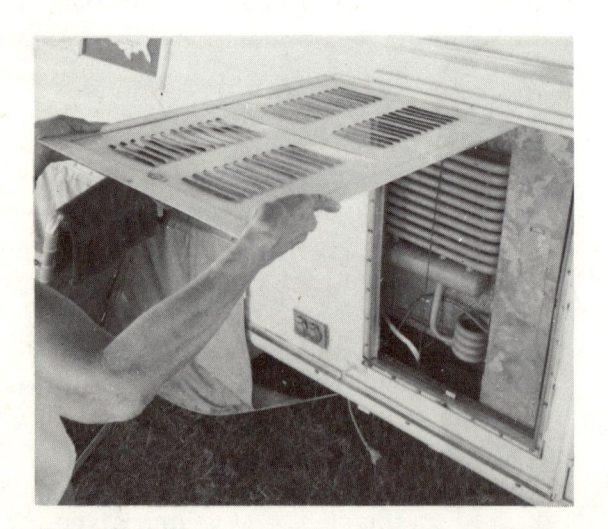

Plate 39. Refrigerator door lifts up and slides out sideways.

Trailer Maintenance

When you turn on your air conditioner during the hot hours of the day, the cooled air will flow under the refrigerator and up around the cooling coils. The average air conditioner drops the air temperature about 20°, so the air that cools the coils will be about 20° cooler than the outside air. When you turn off the air conditioner in the cool of the evening, the refrigerator continues to work just as well as it would with the outside louvers open.

If you have an evaporative cooler (swamp cooler) on the roof of your trailer, it will cool the refrigerator coils just as well as an air conditioner, or perhaps even better. The blower in the cooler blows the air in under slight pressure and forces the cool air up around the coils a little faster.

Lighting the Refrigerator Gas Jet. Since the burner is not easily reachable from inside the trailer, you can't very well light it with a match. Manufacturers have devised two ways of lighting it:

(1) *The Flint Lighter* works like a cigarette lighter. When you hold the by-pass button down to allow the gas to flow to the burner, you twist the rod that turns the wheel against the flint next to the burner, and the spark ignites the gas. After you press the button, wait a few seconds before sparking, so you won't have to spark the burner repeatedly. (If the burner doesn't light, little pieces of flint can get down into the propane orifice.)

(2) *The Lighter Tube* is a tube with little holes spaced close together, which reaches from the burner to near the inner door. When you press the bypass button, gas goes into the tube as well as the burner. You light the gas coming out of the little holes near you, which lights the gas coming out of all the little holes along the tube and eventually lights the gas at the burner.

If for any reason either of these systems stops working, you can still light your refrigerator burner quite easily. Open the outer door and remove the shield around the burner. While you hold the by-pass button down, have someone light the burner from the outside with a match.

Water Heater. The water heater is generally one of the most trouble-free appliances, but when trouble does develop, it is usually caused by the pilot going out or blowing out. The reasons are almost always (1) gusty wind, (2) clogged pilot orifice, or (3) faulty thermocouple.

(1) If you are on the road, large trucks going by cause sudden gusts that can blow out the pilot light. When you are parked, a sudden gust of wind may do it. Many newer heaters have a hinged cover around the pilot, but if you don't have one, you can cut and bend a piece of aluminum to form a shield. We have gone for six months or more without the pilot blowing out, but sooner or later a strong gust of wind will do it. We were parked in Florida one winter, where we had shrubs growing along the water heater side of the trailer, and we didn't have a single blow-out all winter.

(2) Sometimes brand new heaters have clogged pilot orifices, and older ones can get clogged from dust blowing in. The new ones get clogged with tiny bits of metal during the manufacturing process. The result, sometimes, is that the pilot flame is erratic. You adjust the flame to ⅜ inch high, and after a while the flame is much higher or much lower. If it is lower, it will blow out; if it is higher, it will burn a yellow flame that will deposit soot on the top of the tube above it and sometimes will even deposit soot on the side of the trailer. When you try to relight it, it won't light unless you turn up the pilot gas, and then you have to readjust it again. The only solution is to clean it out.

The "blowtorch" type of water heater is used on nearly all travel trailers. A flame like a blowtorch is shot into a chimney tube at the bottom of the water container. The tube goes through the water container and out again at the top, where the spent gases escape.

Some water heaters in trailers have a burner similar to the burners on your cook stove instead of the "blowtorch." Except for the main burner, practically everything in the following description also applies to that type.

Trailer Maintenance 111

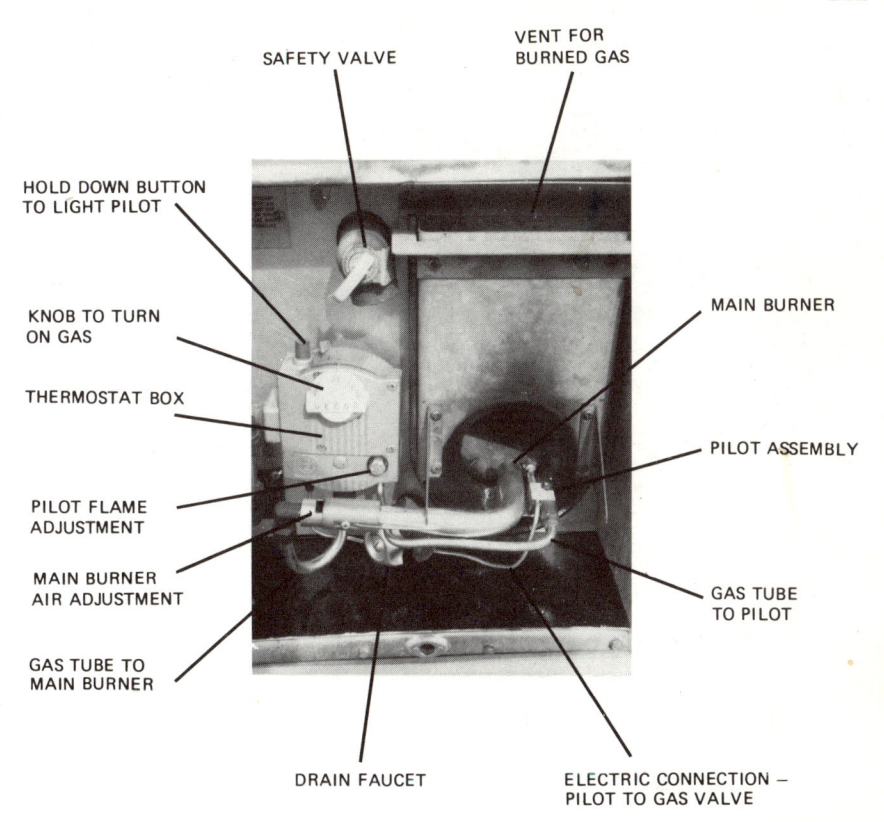

Plate 40. Different models of water heaters have essentially the same parts.

There are three small copper or aluminum tubes leading to the main burner assembly. The largest tube is the gas line to the "blowtorch," which is the burner that heats the water. The next largest tube is the gas line to the pilot. The smallest tube is not a gas line but an electrical connection from the pilot thermocouple to the electrically operated shut-off valve. Just as in your refrigerator and in your gas stove oven and space heater, the thermocouple is a safety device that shuts off the gas if the pilot flame goes out. The heat of the pilot generates a small current of electricity, which flows to the magnet coils in the valve and holds the valve open. As soon as the thermocouple cools off, the current stops, the magnets release, and the valve closes: no more gas.

PILOT

CONNECTION BOX

JET IS INSIDE
THIS HEX NUT

PILOT GAS TUBE

MAIN BURNER   ELECTRICAL CONNECTION

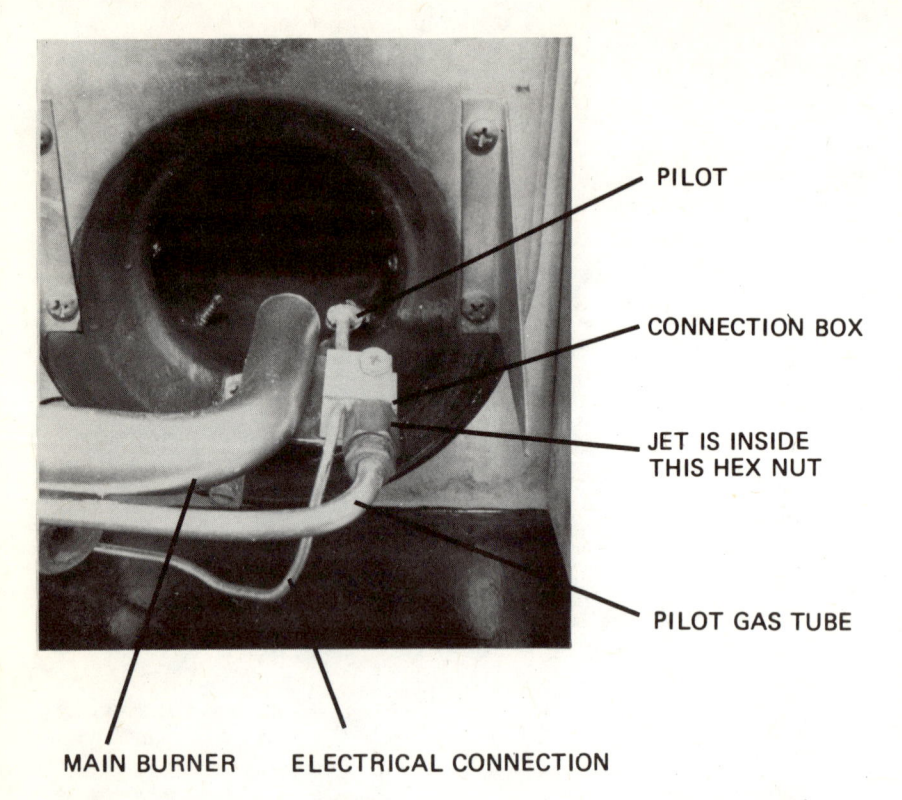

Plate 41. If water heater trouble develops, it is probably caused by dirt in connection box or jet or by worn-out pilot thermocouple. Some models do not have a connection box.

Removing the Burner Assembly. The three tubing lines must be disconnected in order to remove the main burner assembly. But before you disconnect any gas line, be sure to turn the thermostat gas control to *Off*. You will need some small end wrenches, because you will be working in confined spaces where a six-inch adjustable wrench will not fit. If you are careful, you can disconnect the lines without bending or kinking them, so that they will not be damaged and will go back in place easily. There is also a screw (or two) holding the bracket, which holds the whole burner assembly in place. With these screws out and the three tubes disconnected, the main burner assembly will lift right out.

If you haven't done so already, disconnect the pilot gas tube from the square metal box to which the pilot burner is attached and remove the bolt that holds it to the main gas burner assembly. The jet is in the hex nut that holds the tubing to the square box. It is a little fitting with a tiny hole in the center. Be careful not to let it fall out of the nut; they are easy to lose. On some models there is a clean-out screw in the side or bottom of the metal box. If you have one, take out the screw. Now you can clean the jet, the inside of the little metal box, and the pilot burner. Soak these parts in alcohol, which you can get at any hardware or paint store. After soaking the parts for half an hour, blow the alcohol out of the square box and jet. If you don't have compressed air available, use a bicycle pump. Use an old toothbrush to clean the pilot and thermocouple.

When you reassemble everything, you will find it easier if you will first screw in all the connections loosely. After everything is in place, *then* tighten them all up, but don't force the nuts and screws. You might strip the fine threads. When you tighten up the smallest tubing (thermocouple), just tighten it finger-tight and then a quarter turn more with the wrench. It should be snug, but if you tighten it too tight, you could cause a gas leak at the valve chamber.

Now that you have it all back together, brush some soapy water on the joints and turn on the gas lever to see if there are any leaks. If none are visible, light the pilot and adjust it to about ⅜ inch high.

Adjusting the Flame. While you are there, turn up the thermostat until the main burner comes on to see if it needs adjusting. The flame should look like a blowtorch with a blue flame, but little yellow flecks at the end are okay. It should roar moderately. If it roars too loudly, there is too much air; and if the flame is yellow, there is too little air. At the place where the gas comes out of the jet into the burner tube, there is a sleeve with openings on opposite sides. By loosening a set screw, this sleeve can be moved to let in more or less air—similar to the ones on your cook stove. Move this sleeve until the flame is properly adjusted and tighten the set screw.

If the pilot refuses to stay lit after you have held down the by-pass button for a full minute, the trouble is undoubtedly in the thermocouple. Try loosening and wiggling the connection where the thin tube enters the thermostat. It may not be making a good electrical connection. If that doesn't work, you probably need a new pilot assembly. The new assembly will have the thermocouple built in. Trailer supply stores usually carry them, but if not, you can write to the manufacturer for one.

It's possible, of course, that the microvalve or thermostat might fail; but, as a rule, they are very reliable and last for many years.

Furnace. Not all travel trailers have space heaters. Some trailers are made strictly for summer vacation use, and in a warm climate a heater would not be needed. However, if you take a trip to Canada, there are days when you will be glad to have a heater, even in midsummer. In spring, winter, and fall, even in the warmest parts of the United States, it can get quite cold. In southern California the temperature gets down to zero in the mountains in the wintertime. In spring and autumn, the deserts get cold at night. So maybe you should not try to save the small cost of a heater.

All gas furnaces in travel trailers that I know about operate on LP gas. Probably the most common and the simplest is the wall type, which heats the trailer by convection (there is no blower). All trailer furnaces take in fresh air from the outside into the combustion chamber, and the spent gases escape to the outside, either through the roof or the sidewall. The air inside the trailer comes in contact with the hot metal and rises out of the furnace into the interior of the trailer. It never gets into the combustion chamber where the fire is burning.

If there is no thermostat, you have to turn on the main burner whenever you want heat and turn it down whenever it gets too hot. However, the pilot can stay lit, so you don't have to light it each time.

Most furnaces have thermostats that turn the main burner off and on at the set temperature. In any case, all furnaces have a thermocouple in the pilot flame that turns off the gas if the pilot goes out.

Like the water heater, the furnace is very reliable. Very seldom does anything go wrong. Eventually, the thermocouple may get weak and have to be replaced. Sometimes the pilot won't stay on because the thermocouple gets knocked out of position above the flame or the electrical connecting tube of the thermocouple is not making contact . . . just as in your water heater. If your pilot won't stay lit (assuming you have gas in the tank and the valve turned on), try moving the thermocouple more into the flame, a little off center. The center of the flame is unburned gas and is not hot. And try turning the nut at the other end of the thermocouple tubing out and in a little bit, to be sure it is making a good connection. If it still won't stay lit, you undoubtedly need a new thermocouple (available at trailer stores).

This simple wall furnace has the advantage of being able to heat your trailer when you are in a campground where there is no electricity. The disadvantage is that the hot air from the furnace tends to rise to the ceiling. Your head is roasting, while your feet are cold. But that's better than freezing if you are in a cold climate. However, if you have electricity available, you can use an electric fan to circulate the hot air.

Many trailers, especially the larger ones, have furnaces equipped with blowers to blow the hot air through ducts under the floor and up into the trailer through floor grids. These furnaces have the advantage of circulating the hot air very evenly through the trailer. Since they operate on 12 volts or 110 volts, they will work on battery current. But the motor draws three to seven amps from the battery, so you can see that your battery would be dead in one day, or even less, if the weather were very cold. The only practical way to use a furnace like that where no electricity is available is to have a generator. And the trouble with a generator is that it is noisy. Big ones are, anyhow. You can get small ones, sufficient to charge your battery, that are quiet enough to use in a campground, and that might be practical. You could keep your battery charged up with the small generator and, in turn, keep your furnace running.

Furnaces that blow hot air through the floor ducts are slid into the floor of the trailer, usually under a cabinet or stove. The blower operates on 12 volts or on 110-120 volts by flipping a switch. In *either* case, the current to the blower is 12 volts, direct current. When you switch to 110 volts, what happens is that you connect the blower to a converter, which converts 110-volt alternating current (house current) to 12-volt direct current (battery current). The converter is either built into the furnace or is completely separate and used also for 12-volt lights, fans, and for the air compressor (if any) for the water tank.

Some furnaces have a second small blower that blows fresh outside air into the combustion chamber. Of course, this air pressure also forces out the burned gas fumes. This kind of furnace is much more complicated than the simple wall furnace. There are various safety devices in addition to the usual pilot thermocouple. These include switches that turn off the gas if the furnace gets too hot and a back-pressure switch that turns the furnace off if the floor vents are closed. The main blower is usually controlled by a heat-sensitive switch; after the thermostat causes the main burners to go on, the blower does not go on until the furnace has heated up sufficiently to blow hot air into the trailer. If the blower went on right away, the air coming out of the floor grids would be cold.

There are various models of furnaces, and it would not be practical to try to turn this book into a service manual for each of them. An operation manual comes with each furnace when you buy your trailer. If you buy a second-hand trailer and don't have an operation manual for your furnace, write to the manufacturer and get one. And even if you buy your trailer when it is 96° in the shade, try out the furnace immediately. Do not wait until the weather gets cold. When we bought our second trailer (in July) the furnace refused to light. Nothing the dealer could do would coax it, so he got busy on the telephone, and in about two weeks, a complete new furnace arrived from the manufacturer. The dealer replaced the furnace and sent the old one back to the manufacturer, who naturally wanted to find out what went wrong. Had we waited for cold weather to try out the furnace, we would have been a couple of thousand miles away from where we bought it and there would have been delays, complications, and expense getting it fixed.

The Thermostat. One fairly frequent complaint about trailer heating is that the trailer gets too hot or too cold. The difficulty is probably caused by the location of the thermostat. To illustrate: The thermostat is set for 70°. It is placed on an outside wall near a drafty window. The air inside the trailer is generally about 74°, but the air by the thermostat drops down to 68° because of the draft and the cold sidewall. So, the furnace goes on when the air is already warm enough, and it stays on after the inside temperature has risen to 80°, because the cold draft keeps cooling off the thermostat.

The opposite can happen if the thermostat is placed near an inside electric light, for instance, on a cupboard wall next to the kitchen sink. The electric light on the bottom of the cabinet over the sink generates considerable heat along the bottom of the cabinet, which flows up around the thermostat. If the thermostat is placed near the range, the pilot light and the stove burners will heat the thermostat, and it won't turn on the furnace even if the air in the trailer is down to 65°.

If you have trouble like this, you can take the thermostat off the wall. When you remove the cover, unscrew the screws that hold it to the wall, and disconnect the two wires from the furnace. Get a length of lamp cord and attach the two lamp cord terminals to the wires from the furnace. Tape the connections to prevent a short circuit, and then connect the other ends of the lamp cord to the thermostat connections where the furnace wires were originally. The longer wires will enable you to move the thermostat around to different locations and at various heights above the floor, until you get the most even heat. Generally, the thermostat should not be on an outside wall. You can find the best place on an inside wall by experimenting. Then comes the problem of hiding the wire, and every case is different. Usually, you can run it on the inside of a cupboard or cabinet, behind curtains, or under carpet or rubber molding.

Then there is the problem of covering up the hole the wire went through to the old thermostat location. If it is a small enough hole, you can fill it with nearly any kind of filler and tint it. If you have some of the plywood used on the inside of your trailer, you can cover it with a small piece, glued with white glue. Or use a little decorative metal or a plastic button. Use your imagination.

The other two propane appliances are your cooking range and gas lights. There isn't a lot to tell you about either of these.

Cooking Range. The range usually has a pilot light for the top burners and a separate pilot light for the oven. If the gas is turned off for any reason, be sure to light *both*. If any adjustment of the flame on the top burners or the oven is needed, there is an operations manual that tells you exactly how to do it. Once set, there should never be any need to readjust. All you have to do is loosen a set screw and adjust the air shutter on each burner. If the flame has yellow tips, it needs more air. Open the air shutter until there is no yellow in the flame and the flame is about ½ inch or ⅝ inch long. If you don't want to adjust the flame, your propane dealer will do it for you.

Propane Lights. There are only a few things you might need to know about propane lights. Sometimes the light flickers or gets dim. That is almost always caused by a clogged orifice. Believe it or not, sometimes a cobweb gets in and causes the trouble.

The jet is next to the gas valve where there is an opening for air to get in and mix with the propane, just as on your gas stove. Dirt and cobwebs can get in and cause trouble. Blow out the dirt with a bicycle pump.

Another thing to know is that there is a great difference

among various types of mantles. Some are much brighter than others, some give a bluish light, and some a yellowish light, but the best ones are more like sunlight. The mantles used on wall fixtures are larger than the ones used in gasoline lanterns and are usually available at trailer stores. As you travel around you will find various brands for sale. Once you find a brand that gives the best light, it is a good idea to buy a few extra, because you may not be able to get them at the next store. We have found Coleman no. 1111 very satisfactory.

The air intake can be adjusted. If there is too much air, the light will be unsteady. If black spots form on the mantle, there is too little air. To adjust the air intake shutter, turn it to wide open and, with the light burning, close the shutter until you get a good, steady light.

If you haven't used a propane light before, here's what you do. Tie the mantle onto the porcelain holder, which has a groove for the string to fit into. Cut off the extra string and arrange the mantle so that it is reasonably smooth and even all around. Leave off the glass cover so that it doesn't smoke up, and hold a lighted match under the mantle until it catches fire. Let it burn until the entire mantle has been consumed, but be careful not to touch it. After the mantle has cooled completely, put a match under the mantle and turn on the gas—and you have light. Replace the glass and you are all set for a long time—probably. We say probably because you can never tell how long a mantle is going to last, but we have had them last for a couple of years, even with all the jouncing of many miles of travel.

Propane Tanks. Most trailers have two propane tanks on the front, except very small trailers, which may have only one. The two tanks are connected by quarter-inch tubing to a valve so that you can switch from one tank to the other and to the pressure regulator. The gas pressure in the tanks can be over 100 pounds per square inch, depending on the temperature. The temperature greatly affects the pressure, but the regulator reduces this great and varying pressure to a much lower but steady pressure—enough to push a column of water up 11 inches, as previously explained. All of the gas appliances are manufactured to work efficiently at this same pressure.

There are two methods of switching the gas supply from one tank to the other: manual and automatic. If you have the manual type, when all the gas is used up from one tank, all the gas appliances will stop working. Then you turn off the valve on the empty tank, turn on the valve of the full tank, and light the two stove pilots, the water heater pilot, and the refrigerator burner. Next, take the empty tank off the rack and have it filled.

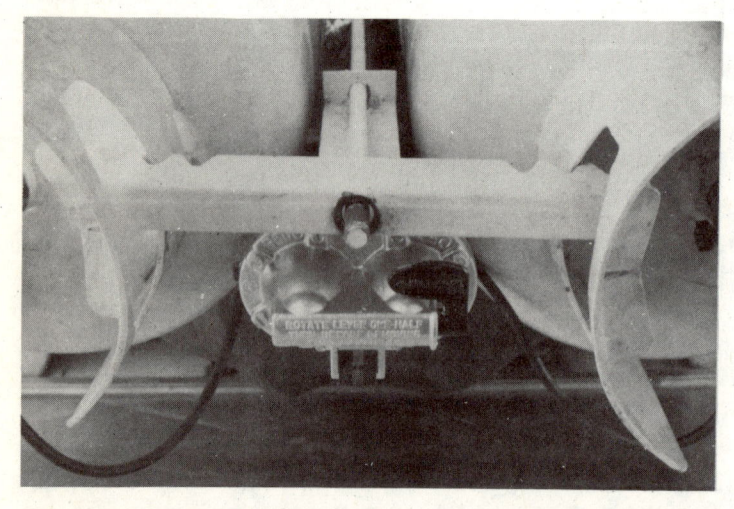

Plate 42. Automatic switch-over valve between propane tanks

The automatic switch-over valve is worth the little extra cost. When one tank is empty, it automatically switches over to the full tank (Plate 42). When this happens, a red indicator tells you that the switch has been made so that you can get the empty tank filled. The handle on the switch-over valve has an arrow on it that points to the empty tank. Leave it just like that until you are ready to fill the empty tank. Then close the valve on the empty tank and flip the handle to point to the full tank. Take the empty tank off and have it filled; and when you put it back in place and connect it to the copper tubing, be sure to turn the bottle valve to *open*. If you don't, when the automatic valve switches over, there won't be any gas and you will wonder what went wrong when all the pilots go out and the stove burners go off while your wife is cooking dinner.

When you are connecting or disconnecting propane bottles, remember that the hexagonal compression nuts that connect the tubing to the bottle *all* have left-hand threads. When you put the wrench on the nut, turn it clockwise to disconnect and counter-clockwise to connect—just the opposite of the way you ordinarily put nuts on bolts. Incidentally, a 10-inch adjustable wrench is excellent for this purpose. Put the wrench on the nut and tighten the wrench jaws snugly against the nut; then give the wrench handle a sharp blow with the palm of your hand to loosen it. If you do it this way, you will never damage the brass nut.

You can buy propane tank covers, which serve two useful purposes. While you are traveling, they protect the tanks from flying rocks and pebbles, which very quickly knock off the paint and make the tanks look as though they have been through a war. The other purpose is to protect the tanks from the direct rays of the sun. When you get the tank filled, quite often it will be a little over-filled. As soon as the sun hits it, the pressure increases and gas escapes through the relief valve (a safety device on all propane bottles), and you start wondering where the propane smell is coming from. The cover won't completely prevent pressure buildup in very hot weather, but it does help.

Electrical System and Appliances
Travel trailers are sometimes parked where 110-volt current is available, and sometimes they are in campgrounds where there is no electricity; so the electrical system has to provide for both situations. Old trailers had just one wiring system, and when you changed from 110 volts to 12 volts, you had to change all the light bulbs. Then, when you changed back again, if you forgot to change the light bulbs to 110 volts, you blew them all out. Twelve-volt light bulbs are made to

look exactly like 110-volt bulbs with screw-in bases and also like automobile bulbs with bayonet bases. However, trailers made today take care of this problem in one of two ways. One way is to have two complete wiring systems, one for 110 volts and one for battery current.

The 110-volt system is much like the one you have in your home or apartment. The trailer is equipped with a cable, which you plug into an outlet in the trailer park and which leads in to an entry box with fuses or circuit breakers inside the trailer. The number of branch circuits depends on the size and electrical equipment inside the trailer. In a typical installation in a larger trailer, the inlet cable would be connected inside the electrical box to a *main* circuit breaker that would handle 30 amps. This circuit would then be connected to three 20-amp circuit breakers, one for each branch circuit. One branch circuit would furnish current for all the lights and electrical outlets. The second branch would connect to the TV outlet, refrigerator, and converter (more about this later). And the third branch would go to the air conditioner only.

Polarization and Grounding. One of the 110-volt wires is called the *hot* wire, and the other one is called the *ground* wire. We are not going to try to make an electrician out of you, but you do need to know enough so that you will understand what is going on in your electrical system. According to the Electrical Code, the black wire (sometimes, but rarely in trailers, the red, blue, or yellow) is always the hot wire; and the white wire is always the ground wire. The white wire is actually connected with the ground. If you touched the black hot wire to a water pipe, you would see sparks and arcs, because of the direct short circuit.

In some trailers, the metal frame is grounded; i.e., it is connected to the white wire. But if you happened to connect the trailer frame to the black hot wire, and you stood on the ground and touched metal on the trailer, the current would flow through you to the ground. In other words, you'd get shocked. When you plug your trailer cable into the electrical socket, the plug prong connected to your black wire has to go into the hole in the socket which connects to the hot wire. If you reverse the plug, your trailer white wire is connected to the black wire at the power source and your hot wire to the ground wire of the power source. When that happens, if you stand on the ground and touch your trailer, you will get shocked.

To prevent such accidents, trailers that have a grounded frame use an indicator light that tells you when the current is properly "polarized"—which simply means that the hot wire in the plug is connected to the hot wire in the socket, and the white wire to the white wire.

There is a tendency nowadays *not* to ground the white wire to the trailer frames. Therefore, connection boxes inside the trailer walls are made of plastic, and precautions are taken when wiring the trailer so that the white wire will not be connected to the frame, the outside skin (and inside skin, if it is metal), or any metal that touches the frame or the skin. It is wise to find out when you buy your trailer how it is wired, and if you need be concerned with polarization.

Fuses and Circuit Breakers. Most trailer park sockets have a 20-amp fuse or circuit breaker, so that it is impossible to use more current without blowing a fuse or tripping the circuit breaker. Sometimes the fuse is only 15 amps, which is sufficient, as a rule. But you just might blow a fuse, so it is a good idea to carry a few extra fuses, both 15 and 20 amps. You should have both fuses and Fustats. The difference is that the threads on the Fustats will only go in the socket they are meant for. You can't use a 15-amp fuse or Fustat in a 20-amp Fustat socket. Some parks have only Fustat sockets.

You can blow a fuse (or trip the circuit breaker in your electrical box) if you overload any one circuit. If the total amount of current being used by all the circuits in your trailer is too much for the fuse in the trailer park outlet, you will blow that fuse. Here are the approximate amounts of current used by various electrical devices in your trailer:

Electrical Device	Approximate Amps	Watts
100-watt light bulb	1	100
50-watt light bulb	½	50
TV (except solid state, which uses much less)	1–4	100–400
Heating pad	½–¾	50–75
Electric blanket	1½–2	150–200
Electric shaver	Fraction	8–12
¼-inch hand drill	2½	280
Portable heater	9–15	1000–1600
Typewriter	½–1	60–90
Electric fan	½–2	50–200
Air conditioner	7–12	800–1500
Soldering iron	1–4	75–400
Sewing machine	½–1	60–90
Vacuum cleaner	2½–8	250–800
Refrigerator heating coil	1–2	150–225
Iron	6–10	600–1100
Hot plate, per burner	5–9	600–1000
Toaster	5–11	500–1200
Percolator	4½–10	500–1000
Frying pan	9–11	1000–1200
Mixer	1–2½	120–250

You can see that if you have your air conditioner on, which draws 11 amps, and you make toast at the same time with a toaster that uses 10 amps (total 21 amps) you are going to blow the 20-amp trailer park fuse. You won't trip the circuit breaker in the trailer, because the toaster and air conditioner are on different circuits. Actually, the fuse would probably blow with even less amperage being used by the toaster and air conditioner, because of other electrical devices drawing current at the same time, such as the refrigerator and electric lights.

Many older overnight parks have old electrical outlets for two-prong plugs. All modern installations are equipped for three prongs. If your trailer's electric cable has a three-prong plug, it would be a good idea to take along an adaptor to make your three-prong plug fit into the two-hole socket. Another handy thing to take along is 50 or 100 feet of extra cable. In many mobile home parks that take overnight travel trailers, the electric connection is a long way from the trailer. The mobile home spaces are laid out for 70-foot mobile homes, not for 20- and 30-foot travel trailers. When you have to use the extra cable, run the end that connects to the trailer cable through a plastic bag or wrapper so that the connecting plug and socket are covered in case of rain. Then secure the bag with a "twist-tie." Put the bag on a rock or brick or something, so that it is a little higher than the surrounding ground. That way, rain water runs off and you don't have a short circuit.

Of course, even if the connection did short circuit in a water puddle and blow the fuse, you could always switch over to your battery lights. That is one nice thing about a travel trailer's auxiliary battery power. We have been in trailer parks several times during storms when the electricity went off. All lights in the mobile homes went out, but we were able to use battery lights.

In trailers that have the two complete wiring systems, the battery is connected to the wires that go to separate 12-volt lights and possibly to other 12-volt appliances, such as the compressor that pumps air into your water tank, the blower for the furnace, and ceiling and kitchen ventilator fans. There should be a 25- or 30-amp fuse at the battery positive connection. If you didn't have this fuse, and a short circuit occurred somewhere in the wiring, the wires could heat up red hot and cause a fire.

We also believe that each light and each appliance should have a fuse in the positive wire next to the light or appliance. These should be smaller fuses, depending on the amount of the current required. For instance, most trailers are equipped with 12-volt lights that have three automobile-type bulbs and a switch that turns on one, two, or all three. Each of these bulbs will use about one amp of battery current, so the maximum amount would be three amps. We put a five amp in-line fuse in the positive lead. You have to take out six screws to take down the light from the ceiling. Then all you have to do is cut the *hot* wire (positive) and connect the fuse to the two cut ends (Plate 43). You can use wire nuts or connectors that slip on the wires, and then you crimp the joint with pliers. Be sure there is no bare wire showing. Do the same thing with all 12-volt lights and appliances. Use a fuse that is just an ampere or two larger than the rated amperage of the device, which is usually stamped right on it. Some trailers have small fluorescent lights, which give much more light using less current (about 1.1 amps per light bulb). Or, you can buy them at a trailer store and install them yourself. They should be fused the same way as an incandescent light.

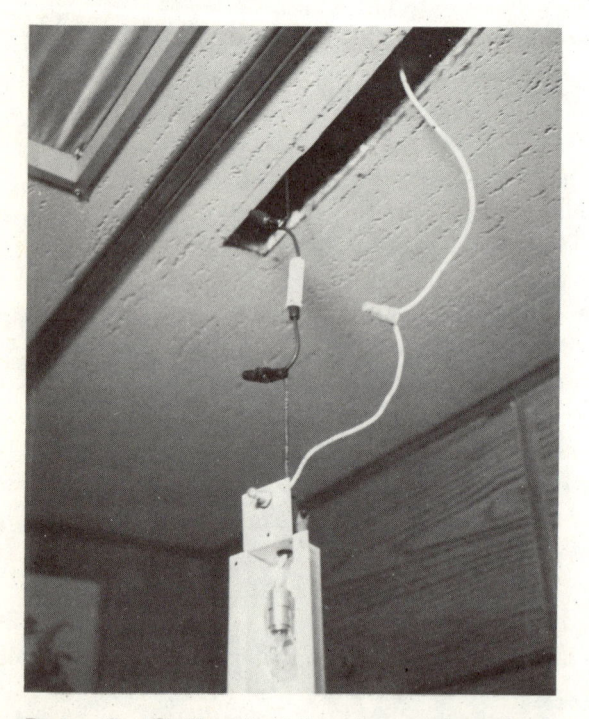

Plate 43. Ceiling light has been taken down, hot wire has been cut, and 5-amp in-line fuse has been connected to each end of positive wire. The white wire is the ground wire and should never be interrupted with a fuse or switch.

Fuses next to each light and appliance are not only for safety but also for convenience. In case of a short circuit, the problem is easier to locate. We have had two wiring short circuits, one in a light and one where a wire came through the metal under the bottom of the trailer. It had not been properly protected with tape, and the insulation wore through where it rubbed against the edge of the hole in the metal. If you have a short circuit and you don't have each separate light and appliance fused, the 30-amp fuse at the battery will blow. When the lights go out, you wonder what's wrong. The first thing to do is check the battery fuse—yep, it's blown. So you know you have a short somewhere, but you don't know where; and it is quite a job to trace every circuit to find the trouble. But if you have everything fused with a smaller fuse, the smaller fuses will blow, and not the 30-amp fuse at the battery. Then, if any light fixture or appliance doesn't work, you check that local fuse. If it is blown, you know the short is right there.

Before going any further, let's explain that the 12-volt system in your trailer is like the system in your car. The battery negative connection is connected to the trailer frame, and that is called the *ground* wire. As in your house wiring, the ground wire is supposed to be white, but service people are not very particular how they hook up 12-volt circuits. The code for house wiring is very exacting, and electricians are licensed because errors in 110–220 volt wiring can be dangerous. A shock can, and does, kill people. But there is no danger from shock with 12-volt current, although you can get burned on a hot wire. So you can't just take it for granted that the black wire is the hot wire in 12-volt wiring. Test it to be sure; it is very easy to do. All you need is a 12-volt light bulb (or you can buy a 6–12-volt test light at any automobile store). If you connect one test-light lead to a wire and touch the other test-light lead to the frame of the trailer (or any metal connected to the frame), the light will light if you are connected to the *hot* (positive) lead. If you are connected to the *ground* (negative) wire, it won't.

Many trailers have a 12-volt outside light. We went to bed

one night leaving ours on and didn't know it until the next day. To prevent that from happening again, we bought a little 12-volt pilot light at an electronics store and installed it in the switch plate alongside the light switch (Plate 44). The pilot light, which uses very little current, lights up inside the trailer when the outside light is on. It is very easy to install: Drill a hole in the cover plate and put the pilot light in the hole (it screws in). Connect one lead from the pilot to the side of the switch that connects to the outside light. Connect the other lead to the trailer frame (Figure 38).

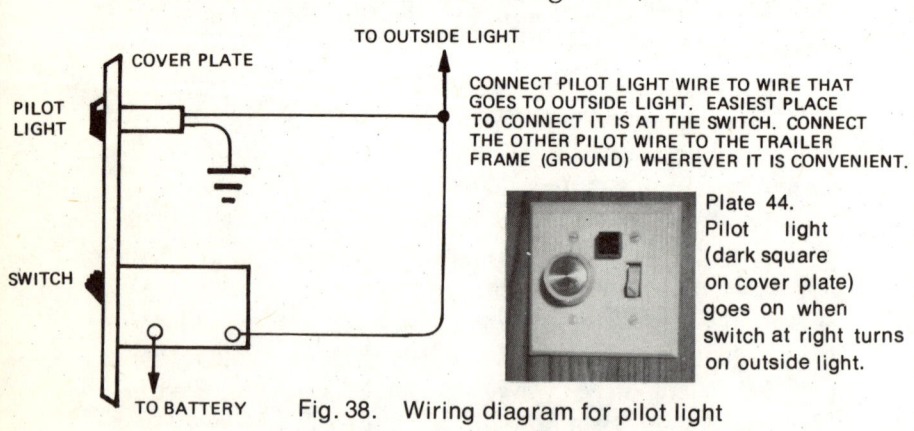

CONNECT PILOT LIGHT WIRE TO WIRE THAT GOES TO OUTSIDE LIGHT. EASIEST PLACE TO CONNECT IT IS AT THE SWITCH. CONNECT THE OTHER PILOT WIRE TO THE TRAILER FRAME (GROUND) WHEREVER IT IS CONVENIENT.

Plate 44. Pilot light (dark square on cover plate) goes on when switch at right turns on outside light.

Fig. 38. Wiring diagram for pilot light

Converters. Many trailers are equipped with a converter, a device that turns 110-volt alternating current into 12-volt direct current. In other words, it converts house current into battery current. This converter is connected to the 110-volt supply in your trailer. On the inside there is a transformer to reduce the 120-volt alternating current to 12 volts a.c. and a rectifier to change the alternating current to direct current, which is same as your battery. The 12-volt leads from the converter are connected to all the lights and 12-volt appliances, and also to the battery, so that it will charge your battery and keep it charged. I am oversimplifying this a bit—the converter actually delivers a little more voltage than the battery. The actual voltage at any particular moment depends on the amount of electricity being used.

This brings us to the other type of wiring used in travel

trailers. Instead of having two completely different sets of wires for 110 volts and battery current, the second system (sometimes called uni-volt) converts the 110-volt current into 12-volt current, so that all the lights are 12-volt lights only. The incoming cable is connected to the converter, and from there on it is the same as the other system, except that there are no 110-volt lights. However, there are exceptions; for example, all the wall sockets are connected to the 110-volt line, so you can plug in percolators and toasters. And, of course, the air conditioner and refrigerator are connected to 110 volts.

Inverters. The inverter is a very handy device if you are going to be in campgrounds where electricity is not available. It does just the opposite job from that of the converter. The inverter turns battery current into 110-volt house current (alternating) ... but there is a definite limit. Ours is a 300-watt inverter, which can be used to power any electrical device that does not use any more electricity than 300 watts (see Table, page 124). So you can't use it for your air conditioner or toaster. But we do use it for TV, electric shaver, quarter-inch drill, electric typewriter, sewing machine, small vacuum cleaner, hand mixer, small soldering iron, and hair clippers.

The inverter is a small device that you connect to your storage battery, making sure that the positive and negative leads are correctly positioned. Then you just plug in whatever 110-volt device you want to use. Many of the trailerites we know have installed the inverter permanently in their trailers. If you do that, you should connect it to the battery with large wires, and as close to the battery as possible. The reason is that long leads with small-diameter wire cause a voltage drop. If the current from the battery is less than 12 volts, the current coming out of the inverter will be a lot less than 110 volts, and your electrical devices will not work well. When the inverter is operating, it gets warm, so it should not be installed in a completely enclosed space (Plates 45, 46). You can put it in a closet or cupboard, but keep the door open when it is on.

130   TRAILERING

Plate 45. Inverter installed in space next to couch across front of trailer.

Plate 46. Same space enclosed with punched masonite to allow ventilation and cooling. Switch and pilot light are on panel above inverter.

Of course, using the inverter will use up your battery, and it may use it up faster than you think. For instance, let's suppose you have a big 90 ampere-hour battery, which means that your battery would last 90 hours if a light or other electrical device were connected to it that used up one ampere of current. By definition, volts × amperes = watts. So your 12-volt battery will have a capacity of 90 ampere-hours, or 12 × 90 = 1080 watts. After it has produced that much electricity, it is dead. No more juice.

The inverter uses some battery current just to operate itself, two amperes of battery current or 24 watts (2 amps × 12 volts). This amount has to be added to the watts used by any appliance, such as TV. Our black-and-white TV uses 130 watts. This would be only a little over one ampere of 110-volt house current, but it is about 11 amperes of battery current.

In other words, to produce 130 watts of electrical energy, the 12-volt battery has to supply 11 amperes of current. Add this to 24 watts used by the inverter, or 2 amperes. So you are drawing 13 amperes from your battery every hour your TV is turned on. In 3 hours, you use 39 amperes out of your 90 ampere-hour battery. Since there is always some loss in the wires, that means that in three hours of TV watching, the battery is about half-charged.

However, if you have two batteries of 90-ampere-hour size, hooked together in parallel, as described in chapter 6, each battery will be only 25 percent discharged. We have watched long football games on TV on many occasions, and with the trailer battery connected to the car battery, we have never had a battery go dead. We have also used the typewriter and sewing machine for days at a time with no battery trouble. The reason we had no problem is that we used the car enough that the alternator kept the car battery charged, which in turn, charged the trailer battery when they were connected together by the cable. So, if you don't use your car enough, you have to reduce the amount you use the inverter.

You can tell how much charge there is in the battery with a hydrometer, which you can get at any automobile store. It comes with instructions as to how to use it and how to read the scale. The hydrometer, which is built like an oversized syringe, sucks some fluid (dilute sulphuric acid, which will attack clothing, metal, or skin) from the battery into the glass tube. There is a float inside the glass tube that rises as the liquid flows up into the tube. The higher the float rises in the liquid, the more the battery is charged. The deeper it sinks, the less the charge. The specific gravity of the solution rises and falls as the battery is charged or discharged.

While we are on the subject of TVs and inverters, a solid state TV uses only one or two amperes from your battery, instead of the ten or more amperes used by the tube-type TV; so, if you are going to spend much time in the boondocks, and you want to look at TV, the solid state kind is ideal. You can get them with their own small built-in inverter so that they work connected directly to a 12-volt battery. Sometimes they come with their own rechargeable battery pack, but you don't need to use it. You can hook it up to your regular trailer battery. If you use your trailer battery, be sure the polarity is correct.

TV Antennas. A TV antenna that can be rotated from inside the trailer is very convenient. When you pull into a new spot, you don't know where the TV transmitters are located, so you just turn the crank and rotate the antenna until you get the best signal. These rotating antennas come in two general types—the kind that mount on top of the trailer, and those that mount on the side. We happen to prefer the side mount for two reasons: One, I don't like the idea of drilling holes in the roof; and two, sometimes the mechanism that opens the antenna and raises it (after it has been folded for traveling) gets jammed and you have to get up on the roof to fix it. If you want to fix anything on the side-mounted antenna, it slips right off so that you can take it down and work on it. However, the roof-mounted type is a little more convenient, as it can be opened and controlled from inside. The side-mounted type has to be opened by hand and then put back up. A shaft from inside, with a gear on it, turns the antenna. But, opening and closing the side-mounted antenna is such a minor matter that it has never seemed to be any particular trouble, and it is practically foolproof.

You can get the simple "V" antenna, which is fine for black-and-white TV and usually works for color sets as well. If you have a portable color TV, you can get a more elaborate antenna for color reception, which folds up for traveling (but it is much more difficult to fold up than the simple "V").

Water Pumps. Larger trailers have an electrical means of pumping the water in your storage tank to the several faucets. One method is to have a little compressor pump air into the tank until it builds up about 40 pounds of pressure. We will cover water pumps more thoroughly under *Plumbing;* but while we are discussing 12-volt wiring and appliances, there are a few things to mention about the compressor. Compressors are very reliable and should not give you any trouble if you will do three things. First, be sure the wire to the compressor from the battery is large enough. In our trailer the compressor ran at reduced power caused by a voltage drop, because the compressor is located at the back of the trailer and the battery is in the front. The small wire from the battery all the way back to the compressor caused a serious voltage drop, so we ran a second, heavier wire under the trailer (leaving the first one also). We joined the old and new wires and put a fuse in the positive wire just at the point where the wires connected to the compressor (Figure 39).

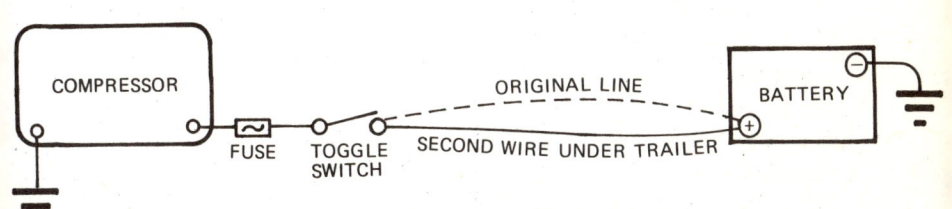

Fig. 39   Diagram of compressor wiring

Second, a tube of special grease comes with the compressor. You have to unscrew the little air-intake nut and grease it about once in six months. And third, clean the little air filter regularly. If the air intake is blocked by a dirty filter, the compressor keeps working, trying to build up the 40 pounds pressure, but it can't get the air to pump.

There is a pressure switch built into the compressor. As soon as the pressure drops down to about 20 or 25 pounds per square inch (psi), the switch turns on the electrical current. Then, when the compressor has worked until it has built up to 40 psi, the switch turns the current off. However, you should have another manual switch in the positive lead so that you can keep the compressor turned off. When you are hooked up to a water supply, you will want the compressor turned off completely. Even when you are in a campground you will probably want to turn it off at night, because it has an irritating habit of going on in the middle of the night and waking you up.

There is another way to get water from your storage tank to your faucets, and that is with a small, electric "demand" pump that goes on automatically as soon as you turn on the faucet. The wiring is the same as for the compressor, but the plumbing is a bit different. With a "demand" pump, you can use a plastic water tank, whereas a pressure system requires a metal tank. Both systems work very well.

In the case of the pressurized system, as the water in the storage tank gets low, more air has to be pumped in, and the compressor runs longer and longer. Then, when you are ready to refill the tank, all the compressed air has to be let out of the tank before you can take off the cap and fill it. The answer is to turn off the compressor after it has run a short time when the water gets low. You will still have plenty of pressure.

Air Conditioners and Swamp Coolers. You know what an air conditioner is; but you may not know about evaporative coolers—often called swamp coolers—which are used extensively in the southwestern states. Both types are nearly always mounted on the roofs of travel trailers. They are made to fit the standard skylight opening in the trailer roof, which is 14" square.

Trailer Maintenance 135

Plate 47. Evaporative cooler. Water enters through ¼-inch tubing in foreground. Lower trough can be drained for traveling.

Plate 48. All four panels are removable. Water troughs are at top of each panel; pads are inside each louver. Squirrel-cage blowers are in center housing and recirculating pump is at lower right.

The evaporative cooler is a square box of varying height, with louvers on all four sides (Plates 47, 48). All four side panels are removable, and on the inside of each of these panels is a pad, about two inches thick, made of wood shavings. There is a water trough with small holes all around the top just above the pads. A small rotary pump lifts water to the trough, and the water trickles down through the pads into a lower trough all around the bottom of the unit. In the center, there is a motor with two squirrel cage blowers that draw air in through the wet pads and blow it out into the trailer. The water is supplied by quarter-inch tubing, through a float valve to the lower trough. A hose fitting on the end of the tubing attaches to a garden hose. When the water gets high enough in the trough, the float valve stops the flow (like the float valve in a toilet tank). The little recirculating water pump has its impeller in the lower trough, and as fast as the water drips down through the pads, it is pumped up again. Water that is lost by evaporation is replaced through the float valve. The starting switch is made so that you can use the blower alone without turning on the water pump.

Now you know about swamp coolers. Why have one? The obvious disadvantage is that if the humidity is high, they won't work well, because the air has to be dry to evaporate the water. If the humidity were 100 percent, there would be no evaporation and, therefore, no cooling. In actual practice, the humidity should be below 35 percent to make the swamp cooler practical. That is why you see them only in very dry climates.

On the other hand, one advantage is that, in a very dry climate, the evaporative cooler will lower the temperature as much as, or more than, a trailer-size air conditioner. The hotter the weather, the less efficient an air conditioner becomes. But the hotter and dryer the weather, the more efficiently the swamp cooler works.

Second, the moisture added to the dry air in the trailer is most welcome. It helps to keep your skin from becoming dry and your lips from cracking. You are more comfortable with a little humidity.

Third, for the air conditioner to cool the trailer, all the windows have to be kept closed. In the confined space of a travel trailer, as soon as you light the gas burners to cook dinner, the burners put more BTUs of heat in the trailer than an air conditioner can remove. With the hot southwestern sun beating down, the trailer is soon as hot inside as the outside air. Steam and cooking odors are also kept in when all the windows are closed. However, with the evaporative cooler, fresh air is constantly coming in, because a window must be left open at the rear of the trailer to let the cool air blow through and out. This, of course, takes with it all the heat and steam from the stove.

There is no reason why you can't have both swamp cooler and air conditioner. We have found the evaporative cooler very useful in all climates. In the humid East, we turn on the blower alone to circulate the air when it is not hot enough for the air conditioner. We also use it when the oven is going or when dinner is cooking.

The cooler uses about one-third the electricity of the air conditioner, so when we are in a humid climate, we use the air conditioner only during a few hot hours in the afternoon. At other times, the blower is nearly always sufficient.

The air conditioner and the cooler are both on the roof—the air conditioner close to the center, and the cooler up toward the front. The air conditioner extends about a foot above the trailer roof, but the cooler, which is larger but much lighter, is almost two feet high. This makes the total height of our trailer 11 feet from the ground to the top of the cooler. We have never found this added height to be a problem. Overpasses on roads are usually 15 feet high or more.

There are some filling stations that we couldn't get into even with a 9 foot-high trailer. But the vast majority either have no canopy at all or one that is a good deal higher than 11 feet.

There is not much a do-it-yourselfer can do in the way of maintenance of an air conditioner, except to keep the filter clean. When it gets clogged, you use more electricity and get less cooling.

The evaporative cooler does need maintenance, which means you have to be able to get up on the roof. The cooler pads should be changed once during the season and the trough cleaned out. Sometimes algae will grow in the wet pads, and that can cause an odor. But you can eliminate algae by putting a cake of disinfectant in the trough. These cakes are widely sold in the Southwest wherever coolers are used. Both pads and disinfectant are inexpensive.

Generators. Before leaving the subject of things electrical, we would like to make a few remarks about generators. We have always been interested in having a generator, although we have never *really* needed one, and we have gone to various dealers to inquire about them and listen to them run. But we have never found one that was really quiet. Some are so noisy that they can be heard several hundred yards away. Others are much quieter, but not quiet enough. We have never wanted to inflict this kind of noise on our neighbors, even in the daytime. We are speaking now about generators in the 3000- to 5000-watt size, sufficient for all electrical needs, including air conditioning.

Some motor homes have such generators built into them, and they really are much quieter. The noise is muffled—a great improvement—but we still would rather not be parked next to one.

However, there are small generators, as mentioned earlier, that generate enough current to keep your battery charged, with acceptable noise levels, like a loud hum. These can be run in the daytime, so there would be no threat of disturbing your neighbor's sleep. And they are small, light, and easily portable. If you are going to be away from electricity and will be using your car very little, these small generators could solve your battery-charging problems.

Plumbing

The plumbing in a trailer is usually quite concentrated; that is, all the pipes are on one side only. Typically, the water tank is under the bed (or sometimes across the front), and the toilet, shower, wash bowl, kitchen sink, water heater and holding tank are all on the street side. When the bathroom is across the back, the pipes are still along one side. The other side of the bathroom is usually a wardrobe.

The plumbing varies, of course, with each size and model of trailer, but Figure 40 shows a typical layout. It does not

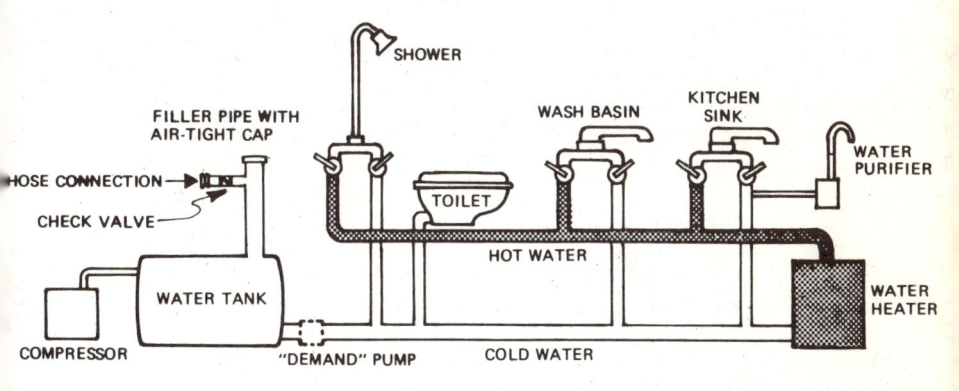

Fig. 40. Diagram of pipes in pressurized water system

matter where each of the units is located.

If a "demand" pump is used instead of a compressor, the pump is placed in the cold water line just outside the water tank (and, of course, the compressor is eliminated). When a demand pump is used, a vent hole is located somewhere on the intake pipe or cap, so that air can enter the tank to replace the water being used.

When you use a hose water supply, the connection must be made directly to the cold water line—not through the tank—by means of the shut-off valves. If the water connection were made to the tank, it would fill and water would run out through the air vent.

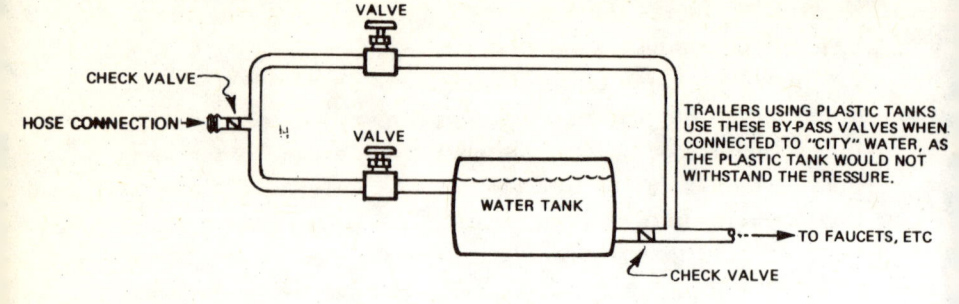

Fig. 41. Water intake pipes with plastic tank

Trailers with plastic water tanks have a water intake pipe that can bypass the water tank (Figure 41). The intake pipe, where the hose is connected, has a check valve that allows the water to go in but not out. The reason is that the water pressure varies. The maximum water pressure in a particular locality might be 60 psi, but when a lot of houses are using water, the pressure drops—let's say to about 40 pounds per square inch. The 60-pound pressure already built up in a pressurized tank would force the water back through the hose into the supply system. Naturally, that does not happen with the demand pump, since no pressure is built up in the tank.

Trailers that use the demand pump system can use plastic tanks, since they do not have to withstand pressure. Trailers with pressurized systems use steel or aluminum tanks built to withstand up to about 125 pounds of pressure per square inch. That's a lot of pressure when you consider the amount of pressure needed to keep your tires inflated.

Most water supplies have pressures varying from 20 to 60 psi, but sometimes you find pressures of 80 pounds, which is sufficient to break an old hose, especially if it lays out in the hot sun. And sometimes it is enough to break a seam open in a water tank, especially the aluminum kind. We have seen broken seams on three occasions, probably because of faulty welding. There is at least one relief valve in the system (on the hot water tank) designed to open before the pressure gets to the bursting point, but in the case of a defective weld, the seam cracks before the pressure gets to what would normally be the danger point.

You are not likely to have a defective tank, but sometimes pressure can get to the danger point because of a fault or breakdown in the water supply system. We were in a trailer park in California one time in the winter when the pressure regulator on the well's pumping system froze. The pressure kept building up to 130 pounds per square inch. You could look down the row of travel trailers and see water dripping from most of them. In most cases, as far as we could determine, the relief valve on the water heater opened, and the water came out onto the ground without damaging the inside of the trailers.

Pressure Regulators. You can avoid the danger of breaking a hose, or even a tank, by using a pressure regulator. This is a little device that screws onto the water supply faucet, and then your hose attaches to the regulator. Some of them have a pressure gauge that tells you the water pressure. You can set the regulator for the pressure you want; 40 pounds is enough. The pressure may drop below the pre-set amount, but the regulator will not allow the pressure to rise above it. We always use the regulator in places where we are not sure of the pressure.

Water Purifiers. The quality of water varies widely from place to place as you travel. Sometimes you get some really bad water. Also, if you have not been using the trailer, the water storage tank can develop a moldy odor. A couple of tablespoons of Clorox in the tank will do wonders, or alternatively, a couple of spoonfuls of baking soda, dissolved in water and poured into the tank.

There is another alternative, and that is to use a water purifier. You can buy it as optional equipment on a new trailer, or there are many models that you can add yourself. It takes out the chlorine taste and other bad tastes, and also some bacteria. We have been glad to have ours a hundred different times. The filter on our purifier (which came with the trailer) is under the sink, way in the back, where it is nearly impossible to get to when you want to change the filter cartridge. Each time, I had to disconnect the copper tubing and take out the filter in order to remove the old cartridge and put in a new one. I might mention in passing that the filter was hooked up wrong when we got the trailer. The water intake tubing was connected to the filter outlet, and vice versa. I changed the connections immediately, but I haven't changed the location yet. Every time I change a filter cartridge, however, I vow I am going to. Most people only change the cartridge once a year or so, but it is better to change it more often, perhaps twice a year. If you are going to be in Mexico, you can get a more powerful filter cartridge, which kills all kinds of bacteria; and no doubt you would want to change it more often. Most of our friends who have been to Mexico tell us that you have to boil the drinking and cooking water and wash all vegetables to avoid dysentery. The Mexicans don't seem to get it, since they are used to the water and have become immune to the dysentery-causing bacteria. Maybe you would be too, if you stayed there long enough.

Toilets. There are a number of different kinds of toilets used in travel trailers, but none of them are like the ones found in houses. The home toilet has either a valve or a water tank, which admits a measured amount of water (usually several gallons) into the toilet bowl to flush it. The flushed effluent goes directly down into the sewer.

Obviously, a travel trailer cannot use this method, since sewer connections are not always available and stored water is limited to about 30 gallons. Travel trailers have a holding tank installed in the sewer line, and the tank holds the effluent. Usually the tank holds 20 or 30 gallons. When it is full, you have to get to a dumping station or sewer hookup. There are dumping stations all over the United States and Canada, many located at filling stations. Travel publications and campground guides list dumping stations, but we have never used them, except once in an emergency. Our reason is that the tank and hose need to be washed out after dumping,

Trailer Maintenance 143

and there is really no way to do this at a dumping station.

If we are connected to sewer and water, after the holding tank valve has been opened and the tank emptied, we have a hose attached to the toilet which we squirt into the holding tank to wash it out. Then the holding tank valve is closed, and we let clear water run into the tank until it is full. Then, we open the valve again, let the water rush through the hose to clean it out, and close the valve. Next, we fill the bathtub (our trailer has a small one), the kitchen sinks, and the wash basin with clear water, pull the plugs on all three, and let the water flow through. The reason for this last washing is this: When the holding tank valve is first open, the effluent rushes down, and some of it backs up into the drain pipe from the bathroom shower and sink . . . and there is no way to prevent it. We have even been in places where the sewer line was partially clogged, which prevented the effluent from draining out fast enough, and it backed up all the way into the bathtub. This is unusual, but since it will always back up a short distance, we clean it all out with the water from the tub, wash basin, and sinks.

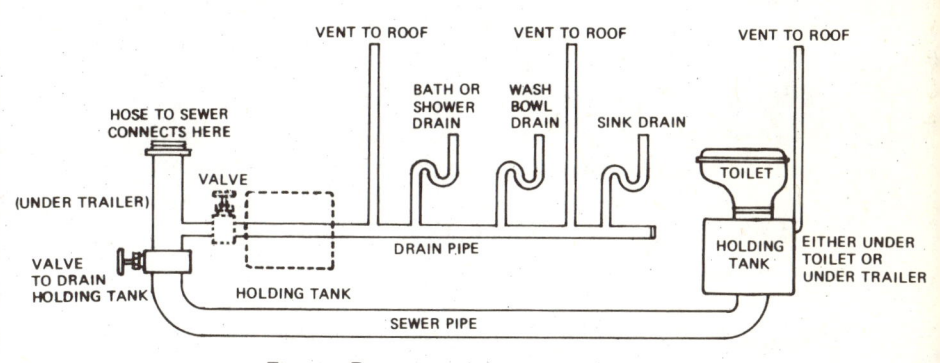

Fig. 42. Diagram of drainage system

Figure 42 shows you how the backup can happen. The sewer pipe is the larger pipe (four-inch plastic). It runs from the bottom of the holding tank to the valve and then to the side of the trailer where you attach the sewer hose. The sewer pipe is full right down to the valve. The drain pipe runs into the sewer pipe on the *other* side of the valve, so that the wash water can run out at any time. Since the slope of these pipes is not very great, when the valve is open, some of the effluent can't help running back into the smaller drain pipe, which is two-inch plastic.

This diagram is typical in that it doesn't matter where each unit is located. All the drain pipes are plastic. They do not deteriorate, are impervious to almost everything, and are light and easy to install. Connections are made with a "glue" that melts the plastic and "welds" the joints together. After the weld had been made, the joint cannot be pulled apart; it has to be cut. Once the "glue" has been put on, you have about 60 seconds to fit the pipes together (depending on the temperature) before it sets. So it only takes a minute to make each joint. The pipes fit into collars and "Ts" and angle fittings, much like metal pipes, except that there are no threads. If you make a mistake, you can't unscrew it and start over again. You have to cut off the mistake and join on a new piece of pipe with a collar. Pipes, fittings, and "glue" are all available at plumbing supply stores and at many trailer supply stores.

In some trailers, the holding tank is above the floor, and in others it is under the floor. There are some advantages to both types. If you have any repair work to do on the tanks above the floor (in the bathroom), it means tearing up a good bit of the inside of the bathroom to get to the holding tank. It is unlikely you will ever have to do this, but we did. Our trailer was delivered with a leaky holding tank, and the dealer had never fixed one. The manufacturer would gladly have fixed it if we had been willing to tow it a thousand miles to Indiana, but we did not want to do that. So I arranged with them to send me all necessary parts and a floor diagram. The new holding tank had to be installed from inside the bathroom, but the sewer pipe had to be connected inside the aluminum underbelly. This meant cutting a section out of the aluminum skin under the trailer, fitting in the new connections and pipes, and then putting an aluminum sliding door over the hole. In case of future difficulty, the sliding door will be very handy.

The one big advantage of the inboard holding tank is that it permits more road clearance. Since the holding tank is higher, the sewer pipes can slope down to the sewer connections at the side or back of the trailer and still be high off the ground. The under-the-trailer holding tank is much lower, and since the sewer pipe must slope down, it is even closer to the ground. Sometimes these low sewer connections are only about 6 feet off the ground and are protected by metal skids welded to the trailer frame. Even so, there is the danger of hitting and breaking the tank or sewer pipe. On the other hand, they are easier to get to and repair if it ever becomes necessary to do so.

Note in Figure 42 the several vent pipes from the drain pipe up to the roof. Some or all of them are probably visible inside the trailer, although some may be hidden inside interior walls or closets. These vent pipes extend all the way to the roof and have little caps over them to prevent the rain and dirt from entering. Your home plumbing has vents up to the roof, too, but they are nearly always hidden. The reason for the vents is to allow air to enter the drain pipes when water is draining through them. Otherwise, pressures and vacuums would form inside the drain, which would cause them to gurgle, and the flow would be restricted. There is also a vent to the holding tank, as air must be allowed to enter the tank to replace the water when it is being emptied.

Not much is likely to go wrong with this sewer and drain system. However, there are a couple of cautions regarding the holding tank. The only moving part in this system is the holding tank valve. This is a sliding valve that is very reliable but can be damaged and have its life shortened if you put detergents (including dish water) into the holding tank. The detergents soften the seals and dissolve the lubricants built into the valve. Also, do not put antifreeze, alcohol, ammonia, cleaning solutions, or acetone into the tank. Such solutions will damage the tank itself, the valve fittings, and the drain hose.

Do not put facial tissues or any other kind of "wet strength" paper into the toilet. Do not put anything in that will not dissolve. If pieces of insoluble material get caught in the valve, they can prevent it from closing all the way. Then you will have a leaky sewer connection, and you will not be able to fix it unless you take out the valve. That can be a big job—and an expensive one if you have a repair shop do it.

When you are parked and connected to a sewer, *don't* leave the valve open. Keep it closed until the tank is at least half full. It is perfectly all right to let the tank fill completely. Then when you open the valve, the water pressure will wash everything through the valve. Next, wash it all out as previously explained.

If you leave the valve open, you will eventually be in for some serious trouble, but you won't know it for a long time. What happens is that the solid matter builds up, gets as hard as a brick, and clogs the sewer pipe. I know of one trailerite who had that happen while he was parked in Tucson for quite a while. His drain pipe could not be opened with any kind of snake. He had to saw out the drain pipe and replace it.

At least two other methods have been developed for disposing of the contents of holding tanks, other than dumping them down a sewer. One is to evaporate and burn the effluent, using propane gas. We have never seen one of these systems or known anyone who had one, although we have seen them advertised. Obviously, you would have to fill your propane tanks more often with this system.

The other method is a new one and quite expensive. It involves an installation under the tow car. The contents of the holding tank are pumped forward and burned away by the heat of the car exhaust. The device is made by a very reputable manufacturer, so I assume it works well, but we have never seen this kind of installation. It is obviously intended for use while the car is pulling the trailer, but when you arrive at your destination, if you are going to stay longer than it takes to fill up the holding tank, you will still need a sewer connection or a nearby dumping station.

There is one weak spot in the drain system, and that is that the dishwater and wash water from the bathroom have to run out. There is no tank to hold it. It has been a trailering custom for many years to put a bucket under the drain pipe beneath the trailer to catch the wash water. When the bucket is nearly full, it is dumped down the john in the campground. (Some people just let the water run on the ground, even though many campgrounds have special sinks in which to dump it.) Since the wash water contains food particles, which draw flies and insects, some campgrounds will not even permit the cap to be removed from the sewer pipe. That presents some problems in disposing of the wash water. Consequently, some new trailers are now being made with a second holding tank in the drain pipe line, as shown by the dotted lines in Figure 42. If you close the valve in the drain pipe line, the wash water stays in the second holding tank. Since this is a new development, the great majority of trailers on the road do not have them, but I would guess that in the future nearly all trailers with cooking and washing facilities will have a second holding tank.

The toilets used in travel trailers differ from home toilets in that there is no water tank. Several different kinds are in use.

There is the marine-type toilet, which has a flap at the bottom of the bowl that moves up and down by means of a foot pedal. We have never had one, but we have heard complaints by the score from our friends on the road. It seems the flap gets out of order easily and doesn't hold water.

There is another type that has a sliding valve at the bottom. We have used one of these for seven years with no trouble of any kind. However, we have taken the toilet out twice and cleaned out calcium and other mineral deposits, which gradually build up from hard water.

There is a third, and quite popular, type of toilet: the recirculating variety. This type holds about five gallons of water in the bottom. A small rotary pump, enclosed in a cage in the water compartment, pumps water into the bowl to flush it. Since it keeps pumping the same water up into the bowl, there has to be a chemical added to mask the odor.

The chemical also colors the water, usually blue. Several advantages are claimed for recirculating toilets. First, you don't have to have a holding tank (but in that case, you have to dump the toilet every four or five days). Second, if you do have a holding tank, you can stay out longer without having to get to a sewer or dumping station. Third, you don't have to use up your supply of drinking water to flush the toilet.

Having used one of these for a year and a half, we can offer some personal comments. The odor of the chemical is not very pleasant, and even with this additive the odor gets pretty objectionable after about three or four days, especially in hot weather. The chemical is rather expensive, which might not matter very much if you are just going on a two-week vacation, but for full-time trailerites, like ourselves, it mattered quite a lot.

If you don't have a holding tank, you can't stay out in the boondocks very long; and even if you could, you wouldn't like the odor. If you do have a holding tank, you can dump the contents into it, fill the toilet with a fresh five gallons of water, and start over. But if you don't wash out the toilet with fresh water each time you dump it, the smell gets worse. And if you wash it out with fresh water, you are filling up the holding tank. The manufacturer's instructions say that it is not absolutely necessary to wash out the toilet each time you dump it, but it is advisable. Our experience was that it is *very* advisable.

Some of these recirculating toilets are made so that they can be connected to the water line for refilling. In other models, you have to carry buckets of water into the bathroom—five gallons to wash out the toilet, and another five gallons to fill the water compartment. When you have to do that every few days, it can get to be quite a nuisance.

Adding it all up, we think the advantages of the recirculating toilet are illusory. And there is a great disadvantage that hasn't been mentioned yet. Most of these toilets have a little rotary pump that is powered by your trailer battery. That, of course, is one more drain on your battery, and if the battery got low, the toilet would not work.

There is a better answer to the problem of being able to stay out in a campsite for longer periods. That is to use a hose (the kind found on some kitchen sinks to rinse off the dishes) to wash out the toilet after each use instead of flushing. Some toilets come equipped with this device. On some, it is optional equipment. If the toilet in your trailer is not so equipped, it is not a big job to put one in the water line. Not only does the hose use much less water than the average flush, but it does a much better cleansing job. With two of us, our 20-gallon holding tank fills in about a week when we are connected to a sewer and make no attempt to save water. If we are in a campground, we can easily stretch the time to two weeks by being careful. And with a tight-fitting sliding valve, there is very little odor. Over a period of two weeks, we would actually use less water than the recirculating toilet would use, if it were cleaned between refillings. There is one caution in using the sliding-valve toilet: The foot pedal that opens the valve also turns on the water. If a wad of paper gets caught in the slide, the valve won't close all the way, and some water keeps running into the bowl. Then the holding tank fills in a short time and the water runs out all over the floor. That happened to us once in the middle of the night. We had never even thought of such a possibility. But it only happened once. After that we made sure all the paper was washed down.

Sooner or later almost everyone has a reason to take out the toilet, either to clean it or to repair it. It is an easy job. If you remove the two or three nuts that bolt it down, and disconnect the water line, the toilet lifts right out. When you remove the toilet for the first time, you will find it a very handy idea to put in a shutoff valve in the water line just behind the toilet. Then, when you want to shut off the water to the toilet while working on it, you don't have to shut off the water supply to the kitchen and bath.

Here is how to do it. Measure the diameter of the waterline tubing. Usually it is ⅜-inch tubing. Copper tubing is measured by outside diameter. At an auto supply store, you can get a small brass in-line shut-off valve for whatever size tubing you have. These come in two varieties: the flare type and the compression ring-type. (The compression ring is called a *ferrule*.) You don't need any special tools to install the compression ring-type, but you will need a flaring tool to put in the flare-type valve. The compression type is smaller, and will fit in a tight space more easily.

With the water turned off, cut a piece of tubing out of the line, the width of the valve, about one inch. Then follow the directions in Figure 43 for each type of fitting.

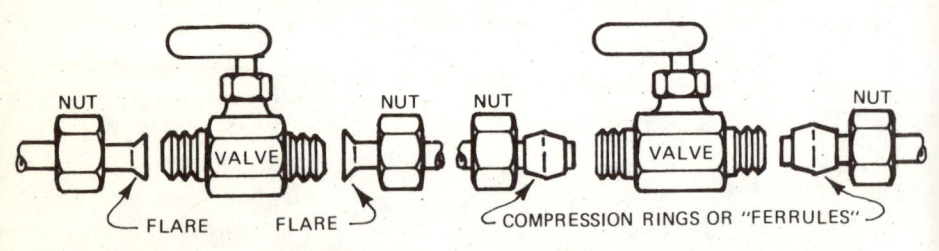

PUT THE NUTS ON THE TUBING. BE SURE TO DO THIS FIRST, AS YOU CAN'T PUT THEM ON AFTER THE TUBING HAS BEEN FLARED. THEN PUT THE FLARING TOOL IN THE ENDS OF THE TUBING AND TIGHTEN IT UNTIL THE ENDS ARE FLARED OUT. PUT THE FLARED ENDS OF THE TUBING NEXT TO EACH END OF THE VALVE AND TIGHTEN THE NUTS.

PUT THE NUTS ON THE TUBING, THEN THE COMPRESSION RINGS. PUT THE ENDS OF THE TUBING INTO THE ENDS OF THE VALVE, AND TIGHTEN THE NUTS ONTO THE VALVE.

Fig. 43. Installation of flare-type and ferrule-type shut-off valves

In either case, turn on the water and check for leaks. You may have to tighten up the nuts a little more. The valves are made square or hexagonal, so that you can put one wrench on the valve and another one on the nut to tighten it.

You can use a fine-toothed hacksaw blade to cut the tubing. File the ends a little after cutting. Be careful not to deform the tubing, or the compression ring will not fit over the ends. You can also use a little pipe cutter. If you do use a pipe cutter, open up the ends of the tubing with the tang end of a small file.

13

Winterizing Your Trailer

IF YOU LIVE in a cold climate, storing your trailer for the winter presents problems.

The first thing to do, of course, is to drain the water tank. There is a faucet, or pet cock, underneath the trailer for that purpose. Remove the filler cap to let in air so the water will drain faster. Open the toilet valve and *all* faucets in the trailer—that will allow any water in the pipes to drain back down into the water tank. If you have a water purifier, take the top off the filter, or at least open it enough so that air can get in, and open the purifier faucet. There is a drain faucet, or valve, on the water heater. Open this, too.

If you have a pressurized water system, now that all the water is out that will drain out, close all faucets, turn on the compressor, and fill the tank with 40 pounds of air pressure. Then open the faucets one at a time and blow out any water that remains. Do the same for the toilet and water purifier. Don't forget the shower hose. If you have the telephone-type shower with the flexible hose, lay the showerhead on the floor of the shower, making sure the showerhead is *open*, and blow out the water there, too. The reason for blowing out the lines is that the water tubing is not straight, and water pockets will be left in all the low spots. I know a dealer who forgot to blow out the water lines of an expensive trailer, and the next spring I helped him put in new pipes throughout most of the trailer. It leaked like a sieve.

If you have a demand pump instead of a compressor, you can blow out each faucet separately with a hose attached to a compressor, or even with a bicycle pump. Or you can buy a nonpoisonous antifreeze and pour a gallon into the empty water tank. Turn on the pump and open each faucet until the solution starts to run out. In the spring, let the water run long enough to flush out all the antifreeze.

So much for the water pipes. Now the drainage system. The holding tank has to be emptied, of course, and cleaned out as much as possible. If the traps are metal, you can pour some automobile antifreeze into them. If they are plastic, I don't know if the automobile antifreeze standing in the trailer all winter will slowly affect them or not. But you can play it safe by getting some special antifreeze, sold at trailer stores, which can be used in plastic. Of course, if you want to take the trouble, you can unscrew the traps and empty them . . . it really isn't much of a job. Or you can siphon them out with a small rubber hose. When you are through de-watering the pipes and drains, leave all the faucets and valves open.

The next thing is to remove the battery and store it in a spot in the basement where it will be cool but won't freeze. If you have a small charger, the battery should be charged slowly about once a month until you are ready to use it again in the spring.

All food should be removed—even canned goods—and used. Start with a fresh supply the following spring or summer. The refrigerator should be cleaned out with water and baking soda. Also, put in a can of charcoal (or baking soda or ground coffee) to prevent any odors from developing, and leave the door open slightly, so the air can circulate.

Close all the curtains so the sun won't fade the upholstery.

Leave all closet and cupboard doors and drawers open; otherwise, condensation may form inside them.

You can do your tires a favor by jacking up the trailer axles and putting them on cement blocks, high enough so that the tires are off the ground. Then let the air out of them, at least most of it. This is the procedure recommended by tire manufacturers. Since sunlight is hard on tires, cover them for the duration of the storage.

This brings up the question of how to get air back into the tires when you are ready to start moving again. We have two methods. First, we bought a tank with a pressure gauge to hold compressed air, up to 150 psi. We fill the tank at gas stations whenever we buy gas, and we always keep it at full pressure, or as close to full as we can get. The pressure at gas stations is usually between 100 and 130 pounds, but sometimes we can get the full 150. One tankful will not fill all four tires, but we start a few weeks early, and every time we go into a gas station, we put more air into the tank. Our tires take 60 pounds of air, so, of course, tires that take only 40 pounds could probably be filled with a couple of tanks. This tank has turned out to be one of the most useful things we have ever bought. We have had numerous occasions to help neighbors and fellow trailerites who needed air—for their cars, trucks, scooters, trailers, bicycles, tractors, mowers, and so on. For ourselves, we use it whenever our own tires need a few pounds of air to keep them right up to the mark; and it is much more convenient than trying to jockey a trailer near the air hose in a filling station. We also have a nozzle attachment to put on the air hose in place of the tire-valve chuck. With this nozzle, we can blow out dirt from such places as refrigerator jets. (And once we blew up about a hundred balloons for a party.)

The other method we use is to take off the wheels in the spring when we do the annual greasing. While the wheels are off, we take them to the filling station and pump them up.

Actually, we have a third method; but we have only used it once, and it is really not very good except in emergencies.

You can connect a high-pressure hose to the air valve on the water tank filler cap (assuming you have a pressurized water tank). Of course, the valve core has to come out first. The water level in the tank has to be low. Then turn on the compressor. The other end of the hose is connected to the tire valve, and you need the kind of attachment that screws on, as on a bicycle pump. The little compressor will slowly fill up the tire, but it takes about 40 minutes.

It is a good idea to check during the winter to see if you are getting any condensation inside the trailer; and, if so, open a couple of windows just a crack.

Winterizing your trailer means that it is going to be stored for some months. If you have a place to store it on your own property, so much the better. Some localities have zoning ordinances that restrict the placement of stored trailers to out-of-sight locations.

If you have to store the trailer somewhere else, there are a few factors to consider. One factor, of course, is cost, but you also need to satisfy yourself that your trailer will be protected from vandalism and that there is insurance protection against fire, theft, flood, or accident.

After the trailer is stored, you may wish to work on it during the winter or spring. Make sure the storage location permits you to work on the trailer and be sure electricity is available for drills and other power tools. It is obviously more desirable to have the trailer under a shelter than out in the open, but if such a place is available at all, it will undoubtedly cost more.

In certain parts of the country, there is another thing to consider: wind. We remember a certain dealer in California who had a number of trailers and campers on his lot. One night a windstorm turned them all over. If you live in an area that has windstorms, it would be wise to anchor your trailer. Trailer stores and mobile-home supply stores in windy areas sell anchors, which are long metal rods with steel discs on the south end. The discs are buried, and the eye at the north end of the rod, which sticks out of the ground, is attached to the trailer frame by means of a chain, metal strap, or heavy wire and turnbuckle. Then the turnbuckle is tightened snugly. You will need four anchors, one for each corner. They come in various sizes. Mobile homes use six to ten anchors, but four should be sufficient for most travel trailers. Another method is to put straps or ropes over the top of the trailer and attach them to anchors, but that might damage the roof. On all conventional trailers, you can loop a wire or chain around the frame where the front V-beams emerge from under the trailer. On some trailers, the frame extends out the rear also, which makes an easy place to attach anchors. On trailers that do not have beams extending out the rear, you might have to drill through the beam and attach an eye bolt. On trailers with the underside enclosed, you can drill through the bottom of the beams and tap the hole for a ⅜-inch eye bolt. Better yet, have a welder weld an eye bolt to the bottom of the frame. The beams under a trailer are not made of very thick metal, so the threads would not hold nearly as well as welding.

Another thing you can do is tie some window screening around all the top vents to prevent squirrels and birds from getting in and building nests.

Finally, go over the whole trailer carefully—top, sides, and around all windows—and caulk any open cracks. The main places where caulking might be needed are roof seams, around ventilators, and around windows. If there are any open cracks, water will get in and freeze. If it does, the expansion of the ice will open the cracks even more. Trailer stores sell tubes of aluminized caulking compound, which is very handy to use.

14

Odds and Ends

Changing a Tire. Changing a trailer tire can be much more difficult than changing a car tire, depending on how your trailer is made. If the top of the tire is covered by the trailer siding, you can't get the tire off or on unless the axle drops down so that the tire is low enough to remove. If you have tandem axles (four wheels), you can run the good tire up on a platform, which will allow the wheel next to it to drop down. One kind of ramp or platform was described on page 89.

If you have a single-axle trailer, you have to jack up the trailer frame high enough so that the tire is clear of the wheel well. Put the jack under the frame at the rear of the trailer and jack it up part way. Be sure it is located so that it can't slip off the frame. Then turn the jack post to raise the front of the trailer. Jack up front and back alternately until the wheel is high enough to slip out of the well.

From then on, it's no different from changing a car tire. If you have never changed a car tire, here are the details: Before you do anything, pry off the hubcap with a big screwdriver. Loosen the nuts, or lugs, that hold the tire on. Just barely break them loose and leave them that way so that the wheel is still firmly attached. One caution: Some wheels on the left-hand side have left-handed threads. If so, the end of the stud will have an "L" stamped in the end of it. In that case, you have to turn the nut clockwise to take it off.

Then jack up the trailer by whatever method is necessary, and remove the lug nuts. This calls for a lug wrench. The best kind is shaped like a cross with a socket at the end of each of the four arms. Each socket fits a different size nut. Select the socket that fits the nut snugly, without loose play, and mark that socket with a piece of tape or wire twisted around it so you will always know which socket to use. Lug wrenches come in different sizes. You should get a big one, which will give you more leverage for breaking the nuts loose and tightening them again.

When all the nuts are off (put them in the hubcap), slip the end of the lug wrench under the tire and use it as a lever to raise the tire just a fraction so you can lift it off the studs easily. Then pull the bottom of the tire towards you until the whole tire is out of the wheel well.

If you have small tires, they are easy enough to lift back onto the hub; but the larger ones can be mighty heavy and hard to lift from a stooping position. So, after you have pushed the spare tire up under the wheel well, put the lug wrench under the tire and use it as a lever by lifting the end of the lug wrench to boost the tire onto the hub. Push in with one hand and with the other hand keep the tire raised with the lug wrench. Turn the hub by hand until you get the holes in the wheels lined up with the studs. Then lift the wrench and push the tire on. Put on the nuts and tighten them as much as you can. You can't quite tighten them all the way, because the wheel will keep turning. Lower the jacks until the tire is on the ground and then tighten the lugs. Tighten one lug and then tighten the one opposite it. For instance, if you have six lugs, tighten one and four, then two and five, then three and six. Then go all around once more and tighten them all again. This method will produce an even pressure all around, and you will not be likely to have a lug work loose on the road. Replace the hubcap, and you are finished. Some people can bang the hubcap on with the side of their fist, but I like to carry a rubber mallet for this purpose. If you hit the hubcap on the edges, the mallet will not dent it.

Storm Windows. If you buy a new trailer, some manufacturers offer storm windows as optional equipment. We bought them, but we wouldn't do it again, since we are almost always in a warm climate. Besides, they are heavy and bulky to carry. Even in warm climates, you do get chilly days, but it is hardly worth the trouble to put on storm windows.

However, for those of you who are going to be in really sustained cold weather, there is a fairly satisfactory substitute for storm windows. Almost any thin plastic will do—for instance, the very thin bags the cleaners put over dresses and suits. Or you can buy it in rolls by the yard in variety stores. The main purpose of storm windows is to form a dead air space between the outer and inner windows. The dead air is an excellent insulator.

If you have removable screens, cut a piece of plastic an inch or two larger than the screen and tape the plastic over the edge of the screen all around. If the screens are not removable, you can cut the plastic a little smaller and tape it to the interior side of the screen frame.

The disadvantage of plastic is that it wrinkles to some extent, so that the view is unclear and somewhat distorted. If you are feeling rich, you can get heavier plastic sheets to tape onto the windows where you want a good view.

Heat Lamp. We installed a heat lamp in a swivel fixture on the bathroom wall. It has been a luxurious pleasure on many a chilly morning.

Spare Tires. Where to carry the spare tire for the trailer can be a problem and, in some cases, where to carry the spare tire for the tow vehicle. We even know of people who travel without a spare trailer tire, but we do not advise it. We have had four trailer flats in seven years.

Odds and Ends 159

Our first tow car was a station wagon that had the spare tire in a well just behind a rear wheel well. We had a bracket made and bolted to the floor and sidewall, just behind the opposite wheel well, to carry the spare trailer tire. This arrangement was satisfactory, except that it took up space.

When we got our second trailer, we bought a spare wheel holder that bolts onto the rear trailer bumper (Plate 49). These are made so that by loosening a latch, the tire swings down or sideways. With the tire down, you can open the trunk door (Plate 50). We like this much better than storing the trailer tire in the tow car. Why not put the spare in the trunk of the trailer? Two reasons. First, the opening in most trunks is not large enough; and even if it were, with the door open, it would be hard to maneuver a heavy tire across the door and through the opening. Second, it would take up too much badly needed space.

Plate 49. Spare tire rack in *up* position

Plate 50. Spare tire rack *down* to allow access to storage trunk. Tire is completely covered to keep it from deteriorating rapidly from exposure and sunlight.

With the tire out in the open, you need a cover to protect it from the sun. Covers are readily available at trailer stores for each size tire.

The tow car spare tire is usually in the trunk of a passenger car, which is fine except that when you need it, you have to unload everything in the trunk to get to it. But I guess there is no way around that small disadvantage. And anyway, you don't have to get to it very often.

If your tow car is a pickup truck, the spare tire is probably stowed on a rack under the rear. If you are pulling a conventional trailer, the rack has to come out to make way for the hitch. In that case, you can put the spare in the truck—maybe. In our case (and that of many others), we have a 36-inch-high cap over the truck box, and we built bunks and storage cabinets inside, leaving no room for the spare. So we had a welder make a tire holder in front of the radiator, which works just fine. We have a cover over the tire, with the center cut out (Plate 51).

Plate 51. Tow-car spare on front bracket does not reduce cooling. A long bolt holds tire snug against the front bumper. Chain and padlock protects against theft of tire.

Even with the center cut out of the tire cover, it *appears* to block the air flow to the radiator. We have had at least 50 campers and other trailerites ask us if the tire on the front didn't block the air flow and cause the engine to overheat. The answer is no, not the least bit. We have pulled our 8500-pound trailer over the Rocky Mountains in August, and the needle on the heat gauge didn't even get up to the halfway mark. We have a 400-cc engine, with an oversized radiator and six-blade fan and shroud, but that is no different than you get with any trailer package. There is plenty of room between the spare tire and the radiator, so the fan pulls the air in around the sides as well as from the front.

Radio Aerial. If you have a battery-powered radio to use where there is no electricity, you will probably have trouble getting any station with the set inside the trailer. The all-metal trailer forms a shield against incoming signals. (Trailers with fiberglass tops will not have this trouble.) However, the difficulty is easily overcome. You will need about 50 feet of any kind of insulated wire. The size of the wire doesn't matter. Thin, flexible wire is best, simply because it rolls up easily, stores in a small space, and can be used over and over again.

Make a circle of about a dozen loops of the wire, about four inches in diameter, and fasten pieces of tape around the loops to keep the wires in place. One end of the loops is attached to the trailer frame or skin. A convenient method is to put an alligator clip on one end of the wire and clip it to a metal window-opening handle. The other end of the wire, about 40 feet, goes through a window opening and just lies out straight on the ground. Now place the wire loop next to the radio and move it around the top, corners, sides, and back, until you get the strongest signal (Figure 44).

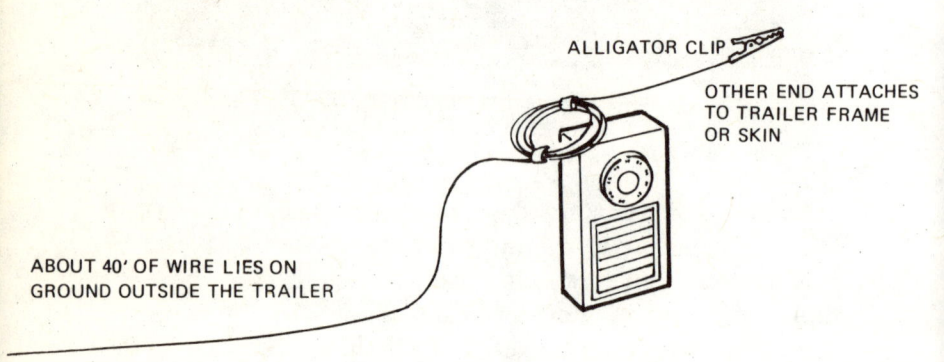

Fig. 44. Radio aerial

The position of the loop depends on where the aerial is inside the radio. Sometimes you can put it on top, or hang it on one corner, or lean it against the back, or tape it on.

Ladder Storage. There are times when you might need to climb on top of your trailer to caulk, paint, recoat or work on the cooler, clean out the refrigerator vent, and so on. If you are in the Southwest and have an evaporative cooler, you will need to change the pads once or twice a year. As we are full-time trailerites, it is necessary for us to carry a ladder long enough to climb up on the roof. We purchased a 7-foot aluminum extension ladder, which opens to about 11 feet

Odds and Ends 163

when fully extended. Then we made two brackets from 1-inch by ⅛-inch galvanized steel, which we bought in a hardware store. We attached the brackets to the bottom of the trailer frame with sheet metal screws, one on either side of the trailer (Plate 52). Two pieces of wood, one inch by two

Plate 52. Ladder storage under trailer just in front of wheels. Ladder slides in from other side and is held down by two metal brackets covered with old garden hose.

LADDER SLIDES IN ON RAILS

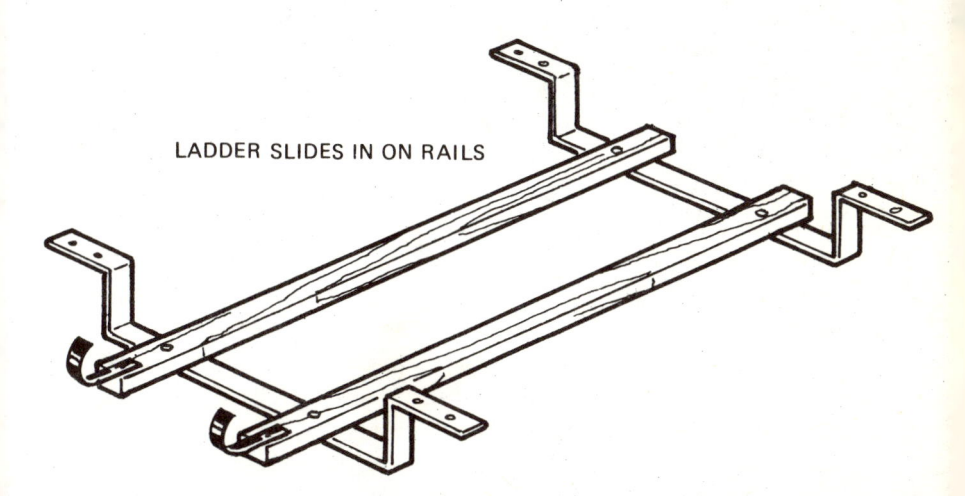

Fig. 45. Storage rack for ladder

inches, were bolted between the two brackets (Figure 45). The ladder slides in on the wood slats. We used two curved pieces of metal on the ends of each slat to hold the ladder snugly, so it wouldn't bounce around (Plate 53).

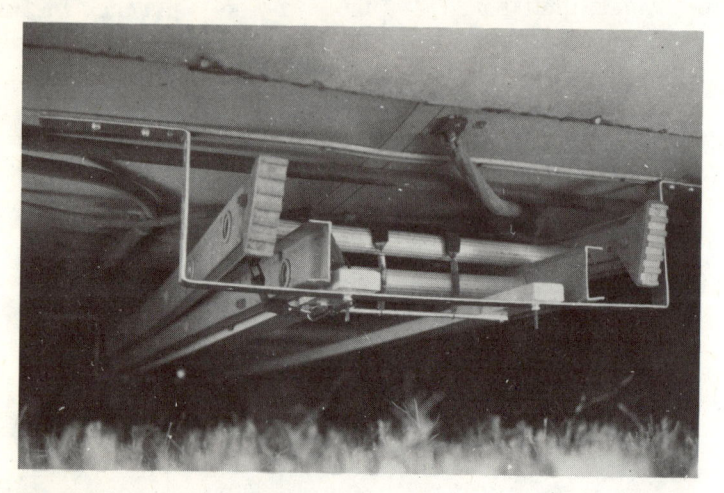

Plate 53. Ladder slides in from this side and is held down by two hooks attached to springs.

Castor Wheels on Rear of Trailer. It is almost inevitable that you will scrape the bottom of your trailer sometime. Many low trailers are made with skids welded to the rear frame, but most trailers that are higher off the ground don't have them. Our present trailer did not, so we bought a pair of heavy-duty castors and installed them as shown in Plate 54. First, the castors were bolted to a heavy metal plate and the plate bolted to the frame with a heavy U-bolt. The metal plate had a piece of U-shaped steel welded on top of it, and we drilled through this "U" and through the frame, and then put a bolt through the plate.

We used castors instead of fixed wheels, because the most likely place to hit bottom is when you are turning into or out of a driveway. When the castors hit the ground, they will swivel as necessary to adjust to the turn of the trailer.

Since every trailer model is constructed a little differently, you will have to adapt our arrangement to your trailer.

Plate 54. One of the heavy-duty castors bolted to beam at rear of trailer.

Extra Sewer Hose Carrier. Almost all trailers have a hollow bumper in which to store the sewer hose, although some trailers have a place for two hoses. It is a very good idea to carry more than one length, because if you do much traveling you are sure to stop some place occasionally where one length of hose just won't reach the sewer inlet. We have solved this little problem with a piece of four-inch plastic pipe fastened to the bumper (Plate 49).

A collar was glued onto each end for extra rigidity, and the pipe was fastened down with pipe strapping. To avoid deforming the pipe when the screws were tightened, we made wooden corner pieces, 12 in all, to fit around the pipe under the metal straps (Figure 46). The ends are two pieces of ¾-inch wood glued together and cut out round with a coping saw (as round as we could make them, that is). Then the uneven edges were sanded off. The plugs were inserted in the ends of the pipe and a hole drilled straight through

166   TRAILERING

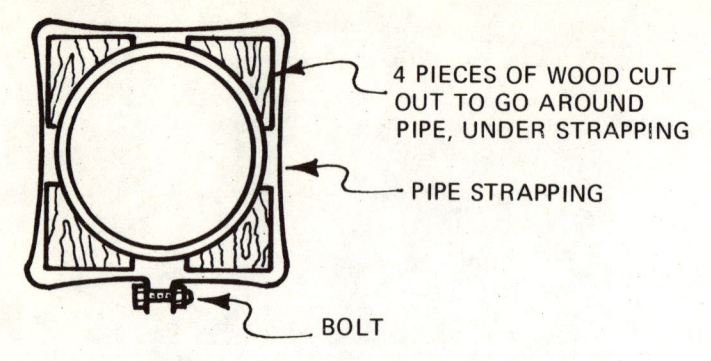

Fig. 46.   Collar for sewer hose carrier

the pipe and the wood. Then quarter-inch aluminum rods were cut and bent to go through the holes (Figure 47).

When we made this hose carrier, we were unable to get white plastic pipe, although white pipe is usually available.

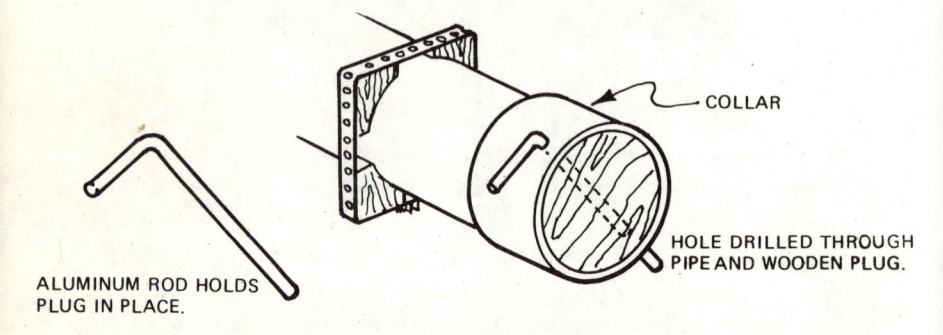

Fig. 47.   Plug for sewer hose carrier

So we used black pipe and painted it with vinyl undercoat and glossy enamel on top of that. After several years the paint is still good.

Ironing Board.   Carrying a full-sized ironing board is not practical in most trailers, so we borrowed this idea from several of our trailering friends: Get a piece of shelf lumber the width of an ironing board and cut it to whatever length will fit into the space where the breadboard goes (if you have a breadboard, and most trailers do).

If space is very limited, you may only get a couple of feet of ironing surface projecting out of the kitchen cabinet; but whatever the size, cover the ironing area with padding and a cover, just as with any other ironing board.

If you are going to be in places without electricity, you can still do your ironing. We carry a discarded electric iron (we cut off the cord) and heat it on the kitchen stove. Not that we do much ironing—any new clothes we buy are perma-pressed and need practically no ironing, but some wash-and-wear clothing looks better with a little touchup.

Protecting Copper Tubing. Almost all trailers have copper tubing underneath that connects to a larger iron pipe from the propane tanks. This tubing can be damaged by stones kicked up from the road. It is easy to protect the tubing by covering it with discarded water hose. All you have to do is slit the hose, curl it around the tubing, and tape it on with pieces of electrician's tape or vinyl mending tape, every foot or so.

We also put hose around all the internal tubing underneath the kitchen sink, bathroom bowl, water tank, and compressor, to keep stored things from banging up against the pipes. That precaution, however, is not absolutely necessary.

Lining Cupboards, Drawers, and Shelves. We line with outdoor carpeting cabinets and drawers in which we store damageable or breakable things. The kitchen cabinets are lined with rubber on the bottom and back, and the bathroom cabinet is lined with foam rubber.

Ketchup bottles, honey jars, and other glass containers are wrapped in several thicknesses of newspaper and taped with masking tape. This is not nearly as much trouble as it might seem. When we buy a new bottle of ketchup, we just slip the old bottle out of its wrapper and the new bottle in.

Covering Metal Clothes Hangers. Clothing hanging on metal hangers will slide back and forth on the metal with the motion of the trailer, and the rubbing will wear out the clothing. My wife has covered dozens of hangers (a few at a time) with sponge rubber. It comes in sheets at variety stores.

168   TRAILERING

Cut strips about an inch wide and start one end of the strip by taping it to the wire hanger with masking tape. Wrap it tightly around the hanger until you come to the end of the strip, and then attach the next strip to it with masking tape. When the rubber has gone all the way around, secure it with masking tape.

Tire Skids. Tire skids are really a worthwhile investment in safety. A blowout could result in overturning a single-axle trailer. This would not be likely to happen with a tandem-axle trailer, but in both cases the skids would almost certainly prevent a fire caused by a flat tire (Plate 55).

Plate 55. Seide skid installed. The skid would hold a flat tire and rim off the road. (Photo courtesy of Seide Center, Van Nuys, California.)

The skids are attached under the springs next to each wheel. The kits come with U-bolts, nuts, and everything you need to install them. It is not hard to do, but, of course, you have to crawl under the trailer to do it.

The purpose of the skid is to hold the wheel rim off the ground in case the tire goes flat. This prevents the friction and heat buildup that so often causes a tire to catch fire. If the tire does catch fire, there is a good chance that it will also set the trailer on fire. And if the trailer catches fire, there is not much you can do to stop it.

It is also claimed that the skids will save the tire. I have some doubt about this, but it might if the trailer were light enough and if it stopped almost immediately. We have had one flat tire while on the road, and it was badly chewed up, even though we had skids. (The other three flats we had were slow leaks while we were parked.) We ran on the skid for several hundred yards before we had the opportunity to pull off the road. The concrete road filed the skid down until it was almost worn through. However, the skid prevented the wheel rim from dropping to the ground, and there was no heat buildup and no danger of fire. As soon as possible, we replaced the skid with a new one. They are available at trailer supply stores, and by mail. Trailer magazines regularly carry ads for them.

Sewing Table. Those of you who are thinking of becoming full-time trailerites might be interested in a sewing machine table. My wife likes to do a good deal of sewing, so we carry a sewing machine. The machine originally rested in a cut-out inside a case. I traced the cut-out on a large piece of ¾-inch plywood and cut it out so the machine rests on it, just as it did in the case. Then I cut the plywood to the same width as our extension table and a little narrower than it is wide. I put pegs in one edge and holes in the opposite edge—to align with the dowels and holes where the two edges of the table come together. In other words, the plywood holding the sewing machine is just like a large extra leaf in the table (Plates 56, 57). Then it was stained and varnished with polyurethane to make it very smooth so cloth would not snag on it.

The finished size of the leaf is 24 inches by 28 inches. To store it, and yet make it readily available, we made a little compartment under the sofa.

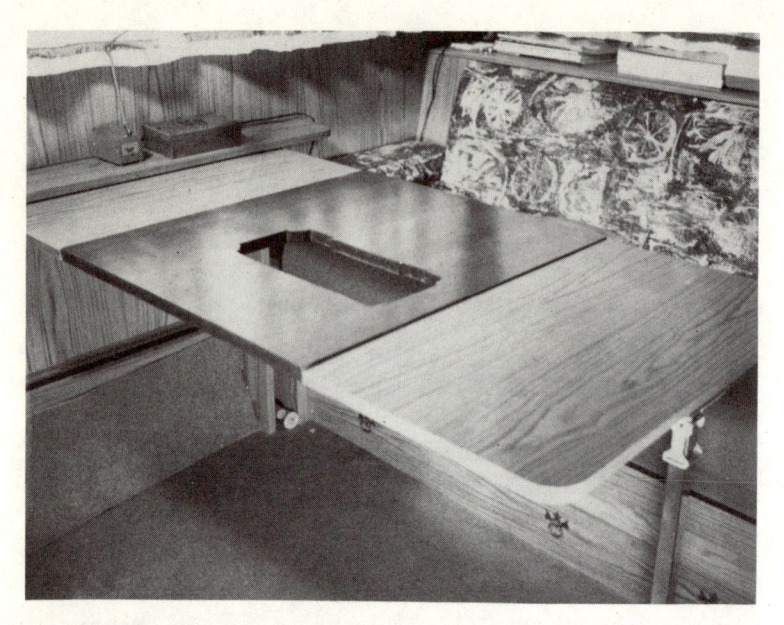

Plate 56. Sewing machine "leaf" in place in table.

Plate 57. Sewing machine ready for business

15

Looking Backward and Forward

During the last eight years of full-time trailering, we have had the most fun of our lives. Everywhere we have traveled we have met the nicest, friendliest people, almost all of whom are anxious to help each other. In campgrounds and travel trailer parks, everyone speaks to everyone. They tell each other where they have been, where they are going, what to see and do, roads and campgrounds to avoid, and where the fishing is good. Many are retired, or have their own businesses, or are farmers after the harvest season. After school opens, most of the trailerites are older people. But none of them are armchair sitters. They are lively, interesting people, anxious to give and receive information. These are our friends, and some of them have become very close friends, with whom we correspond and meet from time to time in our travels.

Our original estimates of the cost of trailering have not been far off the mark. The trailer way of life has enabled us to see much of what we wanted to see in the United States and Canada, to go sometimes where there are no motels or restaurants, to visit our children, and to live in comfort at a cost we could afford. Even in these inflationary days our living expenses have not increased very much.

During the last few years there has been an enormous production and sale of recreational vehicles, which has increased the demand for more and more trailer parks and campgrounds. The result has been an almost explosive increase in trailer accommodations. Private campgrounds have sprung up everywhere, and national chain campgrounds have spread across the nation. State and local parks have increased in number steadily.

As inflation has progressed, the cost of trailer space has also risen, particularly in the newer campgrounds, which have had to pay high construction costs and interest rates on their buildings, swimming pools, sewer lines, water pipes, electrical installations, roads, and so on. Older parks also have higher costs for taxes, garbage disposal, utilities, and maintenance—and the owners need more money for their own living expenses.

Eight years ago, the cost of an overnight stop was about $1.50 and seldom more than $2.00, for a space with electric, water, and sewer hookups. One nice place we stopped charged 85 cents. An equivalent space today would be in the neighborhood of $3.00 to $3.50. If you go to one of the new chain campgrounds with swimming pool, recreation room, and playground, the cost would be more like $4.00. Near larger cities, the cost is higher: $5.00 or $6.00. At Disney World Trailer Park, the charge is $11.00 a day, but that is a special situation.

While these rates seem a bit bothersome to some of us who remember the lower rates, they are still much less than motels, which charge at least $8.00, and go up to $20.00 or more.

If you are going to stay for a while, weekly and monthly rates bring the average cost down considerably. Then, too, there are quite a number of free overnight camping spots. For instance, throughout Kansas there are nice little parks which the state has provided for overnight parking, free of charge, and they encourage you to use them. There are many free municipal and county parks, some with water and electricity. Others charge a small fee. Most of these free or low-cost accommodations are in small towns that would not ordinarily attract tourists. They know that if trailer people spend the night there, they will also buy groceries and gasoline and other supplies before they leave. There are also many national forests where camping is still free or nearly so. As you travel around, you will probably stay in some expensive places occasionally, some reasonable ones, and some that are free—sometimes on daily rates and sometimes on monthly rates—so that at the end of the year, the total cost for rent will be less than seemed likely.

Along with the increase in recreational vehicles, there has been an increase in the number of stories about overcrowded conditions in many campgrounds. No doubt the reports are true for certain highly popular places, such as Yosemite during July and August, and certain California campgrounds where you need reservations months in advance. Our experience has been that there are plenty of spaces if you travel to less popular places or go in the off-season. Only once were we delayed getting into a campground, and that was in the Sierras at the peak of the vacation season (August), where we had to park outside for several days awaiting our turn. Other than that, we have never had the slightest trouble getting a spot. If you can travel during the spring and fall, which we think are the most pleasant seasons to be on the road, you will have little or no difficulty. In midsummer in most places and during the winter in the South, you might have delays finding a suitable space. But if you avoid the widely advertised spots and tourist traps during their busy seasons, you are almost certain to find a suitable place.

If you *must* travel during peak seasons, here are a couple of tips: Try to arrange to arrive at a crowded campground on Sunday afternoon, when you will almost always find a vacancy, unless the camp is on the reservation system. From Monday to Friday, if you arrive around noon or early afternoon, you will also be likely to find a space. A great many trailers and campers arrive Friday afternoon and evening, as well as on Saturday morning. The peak population is Saturday night. A few people start leaving before noon on Sunday.

In general, we feel that overcrowding has been overly publicized and exaggerated. In the summer of 1972, during July and August, we took a trip from Binghamton, N.Y. west through Kansas to Wyoming and Montana. Then we went down through Idaho, Utah, Arizona, and east again to Florida, where we spent the winter. We saw the supposedly crowded places—Yellowstone, Bryce, and Zion Canyons, and Lake Powell—and we found no crowds on the roads and no crowds anywhere, except in one spot in Yellowstone around Old Faithful Geyser.

How are people in trailers affected by gasoline and energy shortages? It depends on where you are, but in general, trailers, campers, and motor homes were not greatly inconvenienced even at the peak of the 1973 shortage. Perhaps they will be as time goes on, along with everyone else. It take a bigger engine to haul a trailer around (you can't tow a 20-foot trailer with a Volkswagen), and there is just no way to get 25 or 30 miles per gallon.

Naturally we have been doing what we can to compensate for higher gasoline prices and possible shortages. We make a list of things we need and add to it each day, but we don't go shopping until it is really necessary. Then we do it all in one trip, about once a week. We take other people with us, and sometimes we go with others. The result so far is that our expenditure for gasoline has not increased, even though gas prices have been going up.

As for other forms of energy, trailers do need propane and electricity for heating, cooking, and light. But the total energy requirements of even a large 30-foot trailer are small compared to the amount required for a house.

Assuming that inflation continues and that the gasoline and energy shortages get worse, there will continue to be advantages for the full-time trailerite and for the country as a whole. Now, and in the future, it will cost much less to live in a travel trailer than in a conventional house—for rent, heat, electricity, insurance, maintenance, and taxes. The cost of travel trailers has gone up, but not nearly as much as houses. Since trailers are built on a production line, the labor cost per unit has not gone up nearly as much as has the labor cost for a house. The same can be said for mobile homes. Looking into the not-too-distant future, it seems that the most economical homes will continue to be trailers, mobile, or modular homes; and conventional houses will become more and more expensive to build and maintain. The signs are there in abundance. In the last 30 or 40 years, the cost of a conventional home (and land) has increased five or ten times, and the trend continues. Not only has population increased, but more and more people have had more money to spend. This is true in most European countries, Japan, South Africa, and many others, as well as here. So there is a greater demand for almost everything.

Those who choose to live in trailers will not only have a comfortable and interesting way of life for themselves, but will contribute to the national well-being by using less energy and fewer materials of all kinds—leaving that much more for others.

We expect to live happily in our travel trailer for years to come, at much less cost, with far less work and upkeep, and just as comfortably as in a house. When we get too old to travel, we will trade in our travel trailer on a mobile home in a nice adult park, where we will have lots of friends and neighbors our own age. Then our children and grandchildren will have to visit us instead of our visiting them.

Index

A

AAA, 86
Air conditioner, 134, 137
Appliances. *See also names of appliances, as* Refrigerator
  electrical, 124
  gas, 66-68, 75, 100-19
Automatic transmission, 55
Awning tool, 98-99, *illus.* 97, 98
Awnings, 87-88, 95-99, *illus.* 96
  tire, 93-94

B

Backing a trailer, 3, 6, 82-84, *illus.* 83, 84
Ball mounts, 28-29, 31-33, 33-34, *illus.* 32, 34, 62
Battery charging, 50-53, *illus.* 51, 52
Battery storage, 152
Brakes
  brake controller, 43, 46, *illus.* 45
  brake fluid tubing, 45
  hand control lever, 43-45, 61
  hydraulic, 49
  lights, 48, 61, *illus.* 48
  resistors, 46-48, *illus.* 47
  surge, 49
  wiring, 43-49, *illus.* 48
Braking techniques, 79-80
Break-away switch, 38-39, 60, 88, *illus.* 39, 63
Budgeting, 14, 15, 22-26, *table,* 25
Butane gas, 68

C

Campers, 1-2, 3-4
Campgrounds, 172, 173-74
  facilities, 5, 87
  guides, 86
  rates, 5, 172-73
Cam-type sway control, 36-37, *illus.* 36
Car-top hitch, 41-42
Cashier's checks, 72
Cash on hand, 72-73
Castor wheels (rear), 164, *illus.* 165
Clearance, car-trailer, 84-85, *illus.* 85
Clothes storage, 16, 167-68
Compressors, 133-34, 139
Connection box, 65
Converters, electrical, 128-29
Copper tubing, 167
Costs, trailering, 14, 15, 22-26, *table,* 25
Cupboards, 75, 167, *illus.* 75, 76

D

Demand pump, 139, 152
Devaluation, trailer, 10
Dishes, storage, 12, 15
Drawers, 75, 167, *illus.* 75
Driving techniques, 78-85
  backing, 3, 6, 82-84, *illus.* 83, 84
  braking, 79-80
  getting stuck, 80-81
  jackknifing, 80, *illus.* 80
  on grades, 78-79, 85

177

Index

passing, 82
turning, 78

E

Electrical appliances, 124, 125-126. *See also* names of appliances, *as* Air conditioner
Electrical system, 121-32
  cables, 125
  circuit breakers, 123
  connections. *See* Wiring
  converters, 128-29
  fuses, 123-25, 127
  generator, 138
  grounding, 122-23
  inverters, 129-31
  plugs, 125
  polarization, 123
  12-volt, 127-28
  uni-volt, 129
Electric fuel pump, 55-56
Engine overheating, 79
Equalizing hitches, 28-30, 57, 60, *illus.* 29, 61, 62
Equipment checklists, 14-21
Evaporative coolers, 16, 134-38, *illus.* 135
Expenses, trailering, 14, 15, 22-26, *table*, 25

F

Fifth wheelers, 27, 40-42, *illus.* 40, 42
  car-top hitch, 41-42
Fire extinguishers, 70-71, *illus.* 70, 71
Floor plans, trailer, *illus.* 3, 7, 8, 9
Friction brake sway control, 36-37, *illus.* 36
Fuel pump, 55-56
Furnace, 66-67, 114-18
  thermostat location, 117-18
Fuses, 123-25, 127

G

Gas. *See* Propane gas
Gas appliances, 66-68, 75, 100-19
Gear ratio, rear-end, 56
Good Sam Club, 86
Ground connection, 50, 64

H

Hardware supplies, 18-19
Hitches, 27-42, *illus.* 28, 32
  axle attached, 31
  ball mount, 28-29, 31-33, 33-34, *illus.* 32, 34, 62
  break-away switch, 38-39, 60, 88, *illus.* 39, 63
  bumper attached, 31
  chain link, 60, *illus.* 62
  equalizing hitches, 28-30, 57, 60, *illus.* 29, 61, 62
  height, 33
  installation, 30-33, *illus.* 30
    bolted, 31
    welded, 30, 31
  locking lever, 27, 59, *illus.* 63
  safety chains, 37-38, 60, *illus.* 38, 63
  size, 27, 33
  sway control bar, 34-35, 60, *illus.* 63
  See also Fifth wheelers
Hitching and unhitching car to trailer, 59-66, 88-89, *checklist*, 76, *illus.* 62-63
Holding tank, 144, 145, 147, 152
Horsepower requirements, 57-58
Hydraulic brakes, 49

I

Improvements, trailer, 12-13
Insurance, 24-26
Inverters, electrical, 129-31
Ironing board, 166-67

Index

J
Jackknifing, 80

L
Ladder storage, 162-64, *illus.* 163, 164
Leveling the trailer, 87, 89-92, *illus.* 90, 91, 92
Lights, 48-50, 61
  brake, 48, 61, *illus.* 48
  propane, 88, 118-19
  running, 49-50
  turn signals, 50
Locking lever, 27, 59, *illus.* 63
LP gas. *See* Propane gas

M
Mail service, 73
Maintenance costs, 23-24, *table*, 25
Manometer, 101-02, 103
Mirrors, side, 81
Money orders, 73
Motor homes, 1-2, 4

O
Overnight stops, 87-88

P
Plumbing, 139-50
  storage tank, 141-42
  water intake pipe, 17, 140
  water pipe drainage, 151-52
  water pressure, 140-41
    regulators, 141
  See also Toilets
Pop-ups, 4-5
Postal service, 73
Pre-departure checklists
  closing the house, 74
  hitching up, 76
  supplies, 15-21
  trailer preparation, 75
Propane gas, 68-69
  costs, 24, 25
  connections, 66-70
  gas pressure, 101-03, 119
  lights, 88, 118-19
  tanks, 119-21
  weight, 7
Propane gas appliances, 66-68, 75, 100-19. *See also names of appliances, as* Refrigerator
Purchasing a trailer, 5-6, 10-13
Pure-O-Vac, 13

R
Radio aerial, 161-62, *illus.* 162
Rand McNally Travel Trailer Guide, 86
Rear-end gear ratio, 56
Rear view mirrors, 81
Refrigerator, 66, 67, 75, 87, 94-95
  gas burner, *illus.* 105
  gas jet care, 104-05, 109-10
  hot weather care, 107-08
  proper cooling, 100-10
  thermocouple, 105
  thermostat, 105-06
Road clearance, 33-34

S
Safety chains, 37-38, 60, *illus.* 38, 63
Sewage system. *See* Toilets
Sewer hose carrier, 165-66
Sewing table, 169, *illus.* 170
Size of trailer, 5-6
Spare tire. *See* Tires
Stabilizing jack, 89, 92
Storage space, *illus.* 3, 7. *See also names of storage items, as* Clothes storage

Storm windows, 158
Stove, gas, 6, 7, 118
   gas shut-off valve, 75, *illus.* 67
Supplies and equipment, 14-21
Surge brakes, 49
Sway control, 34-37, 60, *illus.* 35, 63
   cam-type brake, 36-37, *illus.* 36
   friction brake, 36-37, *illus.* 36

T

Tarpaulin fastening, 99
Television set and antenna, 132-33
Tent trailers, 4-5
Thermostat, location of, 117-18
Tire awnings, 93-94
Tire skids, 168-69
Tires
   towing vehicle, 56-57, 60
      spare storage, 160-61
   trailer
      care of, in winter, 153-54
      changing of, 91, 156-58
      spare storage, 33, 158-59, *illus.* 159, 160
Toilets, 13, 75, 142-50
   drainage system, 143-47
   holding tank, 144, 145, 147, 152
   marine-type, 147
   recirculating-type, 147-48
   shutoff valve, 149-50
   sliding valve-type, 147
Tongue weight, 33, 35, 57
Tool supplies, 20-21
Towing vehicles, 6, 40, 54-58
   clearance, car-trailer, 84-85
   engine overheating, 79
   horsepower, 57-58
   maintenance costs, 23, 55, *table*, 25
   manufacturers' trailer packages, 54-55
   rear-end ratio, 56

   tires, 56-57, 60
   transmission coolers, 55-56
Trailer step platform, 76, *illus.* 77
Transmission coolers, 55-56
Travel checklists
   closing the house, 74
   hitching up, 76
   supplies, 15-21
   trailer preparation, 75
Traveler's checks, 72
Travel expenses, 24, *table*, 25
Travel trailers, 2-3
Turn signal lights, 50
12-volt test light, 64-65, 127, *illus.* 65

U

Undercoating, 12
Used trailers, 10-13

V

Vapor lock, 55-56

W

Water containers, 99
Water heater, gas, 66, 69-70, 110-14, *illus.* 111
   blowtorch type, 110
   burner assembly removal, 112-13
   flame adjustment, 113-14
Water pumps, 133-34
Water purifiers, 141
Water supply. *See* Plumbing
Water weight, 7
Weight, trailer, 6-8
Wheel chocks, 91-92
Wheels, trailer, care of, 6, 10
Wiring connections, 64-66, *illus.* 44
   battery, 50-53, *illus.* 51, 52
   brakes, 43-49, *illus.* 48

brake controller, 43, 46, *illus.* 45
brake fluid tubing, 45
hand control lever, 43-45
hydraulic, 49
lights, 48
resistors, 46-48, *illus.* 47
surge, 49
break-away switch, 38-39, *illus.* 39
compressor, 133
connection box, 65
ground connection, 50, 64
lights, 49-50